HEURISTIC BEHAVIORAL FACTORS

A Study on Investors' Investment Decisions in Capital Market

Dr. R. Amudha
Dr. M. Anbalagan

GRP

GLOBAL RESEARCH PUBLICATIONS
NEW DELHI (INDIA)

First Published – 2011

ISBN: 978-81-89630-29-4

Published by

GLOBAL RESEARCH PUBLICATIONS
4800/24, 1st Floor, Ansari Road
Darya Ganj, New Delhi-110002 (India)
Phone : 23245225. Fax : 91-11-23272135
E-mail: globalresearchpublications@gmail.com, grpindia@vsnl.net

Contents

Foreword *vii*

Acknowledgement *ix*

1. Introduction 1
2. Capital Market Behaviour in India 15
3. Behavioral Finance– A Conceptual Analysis and Review of Research Studies 46
4. Personal Factors and Investment Profile of Investors 78
5. Heuristic Behavioral Factors of Investors 107
6. Personal Factors, Investment Profile and Return on Investments 142
7. Types of Investors and Heuristic Biases 173
8. Summary and Conclusion 207

Bibliography 220

Appendices 224

Foreword

This is a wonderful book, which aims to provide the necessary professional knowledge and guide the stock market investors, learners of stock market investments, the prospective investors, who are keen on investing in stock markets. The authors *Dr. R. Amudha* and *Dr. M. Anbalagan* deserve all appreciation for bringing out this book at an appropriate time.

Today's investor of the stock market has been left with too much of speculations from the market's end and too much of inadequacies at the personal end. More often than not this state of affairs in turn leaves the investor irrational in his or her judgement. Naturally the investors are not given to realize the fundamental need to be rational in their decisions and unbiased in their predictions. At times, this irrationality of the investors is endorsed even by financial economists too.

Thus in the current stock market scenario, many investors are greatly influenced by their emotions. It is quite understandable that this is something that is related to their hard-earned money. But despite their efforts to be impartial in making market decisions, the investors' emotions do have a say on their major investment related decisions. When they become emotional they turn out to be impulsive and hasty in their assessment of the status quo of the stock market and this reflects on their investment decisions too.

Therefore, the need of the hour is to educate the investors to become more rational when dealing with their investments. The investors should also be made to realize that they can resort to professional financial advice in constructing something like an investment plan before they could venture upon any major investment as such. For this purpose they ought to be clarified of the potential personal biases that they might come across on the road to investment.

This book endeavours to bring to light issues connected to the behavioural influences upon the investment plans made by the investors. Embarking upon a logical rationalization of the sources of these influences, the book reiterates that the investors need to be conscious of the same. Noble in their purpose, the authors have done a yeoman job on identifying this issue, solving which is much necessitated by the current state of investment affairs in the stock market. This book is heuristic by itself in that it is potential enough to serve as an eye-opener for not only the investors, but also the observers who are apprehensive about stepping into the actual waves of the stock market. By all means, this book is certainly a welcome addition to the existing reserve of knowledge in the realm of stock investment.

Written in a lucid and systematic style, without resorting to less understood educational jargons, this book will, undoubtedly prove to be a source and text book.

Dr. K. G. SENTHILVASAN
M.Com, M.A. (Public Administration), M.Phil., M.Ed., Ph.D.,
Controller of Examinations, Bharathiar University,
(State University), Coimbatore-641 046

Acknowledgement

I would like to place on record my sincere thanks and deep sense of gratitude to *Dr. M. Anbalagan,* MCom., M.Phil., Ph.D., my guide and supervisor. He has not only inspired me into this endeavor but also helped me in moulding and shaping this thesis to its present form.

I gratefully record my deep sense of gratitude to the members of the Doctoral Committee *Dr. A.R. Veeramani,* Registrar i/c, Thiruvalluvar University, Vellore and *Dr. Mohammed Galib Hussain*, Professor and Head, Department of Corporate Secretaryship, Islamiah College, Vaniyambadi. But for their constructive criticisms and contributions during the research progress review meetings of the Doctoral Committee, this work would have not taken its present form.

I feel immense pleasure in expressing my profound regards and gratitude to *Thiru. G. Viswanathan,* Founder and Chancellor, VIT University, for his incessant encouragement in my academic endeavors to complete my research in Commerce and Management.

I am deeply indebted to *Dr. B. Venkatachalam,* MD, Hexagon Capital Markets Ltd., Bangalore, for his valuable guidance and constant support to complete the research programme and also acknowledged with great encomiums for providing with required secondary data for this study.

I am extremely thankful to *Mr. Prabhakar,* Bangalore Stock Exchange, for facilitating in collection of necessary data for this study.

I would like to thank *Dr. D. Daniel Ezhilarasu,* Principal, Voorhees College, Vellore, for giving me this opportunity to pursue the research programme in Thiruvalluvar University through Voorhees College.

My special thanks to *Dr. Christopher,* Sacred Heart College, who was instrumental in helping with my data analysis and interpretation.

I thank my beloved son, *R.S. Dinesh Kumar,* for bearing the pains and sacrifice made, due to my absence at home, during my study period. These prized persons who had been extending help and support in one way or other in completion of my research work, always remain indelible in my memory forever my life.

Above all, I THANK THE ALMIGHTY for his bountiful blessings to make this happen.

I join with my co-author to record our appreciation and sincere thanks to M/s Global Research Publications for undertaking the responsibility to bring out this book in a short duration in an elegant manner.

R. AMUDHA

1

Introduction

Human Beings are motivated by self-interest and tend to make rational decisions, especially in the field of their investment. Most of the investment decisions in the world are based (or biased) on some of the mental attitudes such as emotions, sentiments and feelings of investors. DeBondt and Thaler (1995), argue that a good psychological finance theory will be grounded on psychological evidence about how people actually behave. Such a theory should allow to concur the rational side of investor decisions. To deserve consideration a theory should be parsimonious, explaining a range of anomalous patterns in different contexts, and generate new empirical implications. In this context a few attempts have been made to develop a comprehensive theory for the securities market, based on the behavior of the investors' rationality in decisions.

The field of Behavioral Finance emerged to believe that individuals behave in a rational manner and that all existing information is supposed to be embedded in the investment process. This assumption is the crux of the financial theory EMH (Efficient Market Hypothesis) formulated by Eugene Fama in 1970. The theory suggests that at any given time , stock prices fully reflect all available information on a particular stock and / or market, and an investor has a role in predicting a return on a stock price to 'out-profit' others in the market and when it comes to money and investing, investors are always rational in their decisions. Subsequently, several researchers questioned the validity of this assumption and have uncovered evidences that rational behavior is not always as prevalent as it was believed. Hence, Behavioral Finance attempts to understand and explain how human 'emotions' influence investors in their decision-making process, which end up to be irrational.

Insight into the theory and findings of Behavioral Finance explains, how, every investor is distinct and unique, with different financial goals, varied level of risk-taking, different perceptions about the market or industry or corporate etc. Such decisions in ultimatum, taken by the investor's, affects the stock market in the short run, resulting either in over or under-valuation of the stock prices. Behavioral Scientists argue that investors often behave irrationally, producing inefficient markets and mispriced securities in the process of making money. But, consistently uncovering these inefficiencies so as to manage investments, effectively and economically, has been a challenging question of the Behavioral theorists.

Many of the mispricings in the financial markets cannot be detected because market participants do not fully understand many factors that influence prices of financial securities. The patterns of security markets reflect the heterogeneity in information processing by the investment public (DeBondt and Thaler,1985 ; Jagadeesh and Titman, 1993; Lee and Swaminathan, 2000) . Several instances in the capital market history has a common phenomenon of short-term trends followed by a longer run trend and a trend reversal leading to a price convergence or a market correction[1], due to the interplay of various cognitive biases such as Overconfidence, Availability Bias, Contagious Enthusiasm etc. As prices move upward, investors who had bought those stocks are vindicated to believe that they have expertise in capital market. This would lure substantial number of new investors who might start investing on borrowed funds, increasing the trade volumes thereby forcing an upward trend triggered by 'availability bias' or / and 'recency bias'. The future predictions on an upward movement is also optimistic to add to the volumes. But then creeps in the 'loss aversion' or 'intuitive feeling', which pulls back the reins, with an expectation of a fall in the trend causing a reversal or a correction.

Statement of Problem

In the Post liberalization period, India witnessed tremendous uptrend in terms of volume and value of transactions, in the day-to-day stock market operations. Business growth in the Capital market segment jumped by leaps and bounds especially in 2007 & 2008. This paradigm shift is contributed by advancement of technology in the stock market mechanisms and financial operations. More number of players (stock traders and intermediaries) entered the stock market, equity cult enhanced in Tier 2 and Tier 3 cities attracting more number of investors, contribution of GDP from various sectors and huge inflow of foreign capital into India were the major changes.

The above developments enabled ease in trading operations, setting up of trading terminals anywhere at any place, decrease of the trading costs (from two and half percent to 0.25 percent - almost around 80 percent), and infusion of Knowledge Capital. The substantial shift from manufacturing and agriculture towards the service sector churned out a knowledge-based economy, constituting the technically equipped, well educated intellectual young mass, who were catalytic in diverting their surplus funds into the Indian Capital market, facilitating an empowered economy. These factors were some of the economic reasons which increased the capital market turnover but at the same time, such increase also had an impact of the investors' behaviour[2].

Among the various traits, the major traits influencing the investor's decision-making process are 'Heuristics - Driven biases'. Some research studies in India has been conducted on various anomalies in the stock market but not much in 'heuristics'. Hence a study on 'heuristics' in Indian context was in need to find out whether the 'heuristics' behaviour of the investors' is influencing the decision-making process or not.

The concept Heuristics was introduced by Daniel Kahneman and Amos Tversky and conducted research in developed countries. India being a developing country, the knowledge level, the information diffusion, the cultural values etc. are highly different from the western countries. Within the country, we find the people, unified by varied culture and sentiments. Also, the Indians are identified to be highly prone to emotions, sentiments and feelings. These behavioral and cultural values with a high level of sentimental values do have influence on the investment decisions. The cognitive biases normally vary with the level of risk taken by the investors, and scanty attempt have been made to analyse the intensity of such heuristics, dominating the Behavioral Patterns of investors. The investors seem to exhibit a wide variation in their Expected returns and the Average earned returns[3]. The new entrants in the capital market, generally have a strong expectation of a higher range of Expected returns. At the same time, it appears that the irrationality and heuristic behavior had been an impediment to achieve their expected targets, due to which their actual Earned Returns are substantially low and at times with negative returns. Many investors usually admit their losses with much reluctance, but do not retreat from market, anticipating to capture what they have lost.

Finally, it is quiet common that the investor's prefer with a rational / irrational choice to join the crowd rather than to beat the market. The investor sentiments will not spare even the sophisticated traders, however rational their decisions may be, they cannot escape the wrath of the biased errors. May be the informed investors intensity of rationality in decisions are better than the uninformed investors, but none are free from the biases in their investment decisions.

A study is desirable, to identify the heuristic factors influencing the financial decisions and to categorize the investors into some types based on the level of acceptance of risk in their investments in capital market and to find out the prominent characteristics specific to the heuristic behavior that is dominating in each of the designated category of investors. Therefore, this study is an attempt, in this direction to expose the heuristics influencing the behavior of investors in the Indian Market conditions.

Objectives of the Study

1. To portray the conceptual and theoretical backdrop for the study of Heuristics in Behavioral Finance.
2. To examine the personal factors and investment profile of the investors.
3. To analyse the relationship between personal factors and investment profile with Investors' Risk-Taking capacity..
4. To identify the heuristic factors that influences the investors' decision making in their investments.
5. To associate the personal and investment profile of investors with the Returns Earned on their investments.
6. To examine the relationship between the types of investors and the heuristic-driven biases.

The Hypothesis Tested

The following hypothesis were felt pertinent to be tested

H_1 : There is no relationship between the personal factors and the investors' risk-taking capacity.

H_2 : The investment profile of the investors does not have any relationship with the Investors' risk-taking capacity.

H_3 : The personal factors do not have any significant relationship with the Earned Returns of the Investors.

H_4 : There does not exist any significant relationship between investment profile of investors with their Earned returns on investment.

H_5 : The types of investors are not influenced by any of the identified heuristic biases.

Research Design & Methodology

Nature of Study: This is an exploratory study. The study is about the behavioral biases in investment decisions influencing the Earned Return of the investors. The investors of stock market are the respondents for this study. The investors are broadly classified into three types based on their nature and level of risk-taken by them in their investments, in addition to their application of analytical skills. The study attempts to analyse the relationship on their earned return with the investor category, influenced by the behavioral biases or heuristics. The study involved three stages. The first stage was set to delineate the study areas, select the respondents, and defining of the independent variables. The second stage was to conduct the field work for collecting the necessary information. The third stage of the study involved statistical analysis and interpretation of the findings.

Sources of Data

The data collected includes primary data basically through a questionnaire designed to obtain information from the investors in the stock market, collectively from Institutional Investors, retail investors, Intermediary Investors, day traders, involved in trading either for their own account or on behalf of their clients, and investment/fund managers. The demography of the sample under research has been confined to Bangalore city only. Bangalore is a city with population representing the people of all parts of India and the investors of Bangalore stock market is assumed to be heterogeneous in character. The demography of the sampling unit was chosen based on the increased awareness of the stock market industry in recent years, strong interest of potential investors due to increase in the income level especially of those in the IT companies, with redundant purchasing power at their disposal, the booming entrepreneur class, and flourishing business enterprises and more women normally housewives entering into the stock market business during the study period 2005- 2007.

The Bangalore Stock Exchange had 124 Individual Members and 118 corporate Members in the year 2005*. Out of this, the questionnaires were distributed to 105 individual members, who were the residents of Bangalore and to 30 corporate members (or intermediaries), sorted out, of those having corporate offices in Bangalore, also the registered members of both BSE and NSE and interested in responding. Apart from the registered members of Bangalore Stock Exchange, Portfolio Managers from five (public and private sector) banks were selected for data collection. For all the 30 corporate members chosen, 10 questionnaires were distributed to those investors, selected from the list obtained from the respective stock broking firm. The selection of investors of the corporate members and portfolio managers, were based cn convenience sampling.

From the sampling frame, of 410, the responses accounted for a total of 328. Out of which, the final sample consisted of 300 responses which were complete and usable for the study. The response rate of 75% is considered satisfactory in view of the experience of the previous researchers.

The Instrument

The Research Strategy adopted was Survey Method, from a sample of 300 respondents, who were mainly the investors in the stock market. The Data Collection is through self-administered questionnaire and scheduling the interactive interview process with those respondents who were available in their respective office premises during the trading hours, for understanding the variables of the Investor Behavior Pattern as also to obtain the first-hand information about their experience and observe on their emotive decisions taken at the time of trading hours.

A questionnaire was developed to identify the behavioral biases and to ascertain the intensity or level of risk taken by the investors. An inventory of behavioral attributes in investment decisions has been built, and 50 statements have been developed to assess the behavioral traits of investors.

Part A of the questionnaire contains 16 closed-end questions, to assess the Demographic and Investment Variables such as Age, Type of Investments, Education, Occupation, Profession, Tenure of Investment, Expected and Average Return of Investment, Level of Risk-Taking, Income Level, Value of Investments, Judgment on investment decisions etc.

Part B of the questionnaire contains 49 statements in a 5 point Likert Scale, to identify and probe through the behavioral biases in the decisions taken by the investors, constructed with scales as Strongly Agree (SA), Agree (A) , No opinion (NO), Disagree (D), and Strongly Disagree (SD).

Pilot Study

The questionnaire was sent to 10 experts in the area of Finance and Psychology to obtain their views on the design of the study. The modifications suggested by six of the experts who had responded the request, to opine on the validity of the questionnaire, has been duly incorporated.

A draft questionnaire was administered to a selected group of 50 respondents in Bangalore. On the basis of the comments received from the investors, the final questionnaire has been prepared after making the language less technical and communicable to the respondents in the stock market for data collection.

Sample Design and Sample Size

The researcher adopted stratified simple random sampling method. The respondents chosen for the study were from an age group ranging from 20 years to 65 years, in Bangalore city including in itself the different strata of investors like students, Investment & Fund Managers, Retired salaried class and businessmen, Stock Brokers, and Investment Advisors. The questionnaire was distributed to 410 respondents, of different strata classified as Individual members, Corporate members and Portfolio managers. The selection of investors from each corporate member were according to convenience sampling, chosen from the list provided by each corporate member, and the response was obtained from 328 respondents. Out of which 28 questionnaires were found to be incomplete, and so discarded for analysis of the study. Hence, the final sample was 300 responses which were complete and usable, taken for analysis of this study.

Reliability Tests

Besides ensuring the validity of the instrument, that is to be guided in a study using qualitative methodology, Reliability tests were made.

The Reliability analysis using Cronbach's Alpha scale were tested on the demographic variables of the respondents, showed a reliability of .741 given in Table 1, which is greater than .5 confirming the adequacy and authenticity of the questionnaire, which is considered as highly significant.

Table 1
Reliability Statistics

Cronbach's Alpha	*N of Items*
.741	287

Table 2
Scale Statistics

Mean	*Variance*	*Std. Variation*	*N of Items*
109.4	179.29	13.3900	49

Statistical Tools and Analysis

The statistical tools used in this study, to test the behavior of the investors in Stock market, includes the percentage analysis, Factor Analysis using KMO & Barlett's Test, Principal Component Analysis, Rotated Component Matrix, Chi-Square and ANOVA .

The collected data were edited, coded and summarized with the help of the Statistical package. The statistical tools such as percentage analysis, Factor Analysis, Regression analysis, and ANOVA were used in this study for analyzing the data. Factor analysis was applied to identify the heuristic factors. Chi-square was used to analyse significant relationship between the two variables under consideration relating to personal and Investment factors with Basic Nature of Investors. Spearman correlation was applied to measure the degree of correlation between the Nature of Investors based on their risk capacity and their personal and investment profile. ANOVA was used to examine the relationship of the Average Returns Earned by investors during the study period based on their personal and investment factors and the Regression analysis was used to assess the existence of multiple correlation among the eight heuristic factors in association with the Type of investors. The Rank Correlation was applied to know the investor's priority on their investments made.

Significance of the Study

Studies relating to Investors' decisions in stock market, affected by the heuristic behavior, is in scanty, in the area of Behavioral Finance, especially in the Indian context. A study to explore the cognitive biases in decision-making, which could provide suggestions to improvise the behavioral characteristics so as to minimize the errors in decisions, may help investors at a great extent. Focusing on this aspect, this research study has been an attempt to understand the biasness in decisions, caused due to the psychological attributes affecting the behavior of the investors.

The significance of the study is to identify the heuristic biases exhibited by the investors, by choosing from a group of behavioral statements, which might induce on the investors' decisions. For this purpose, the investors are categorized into three types framed, from their personal and investment profile.

Considering the above, the study attempts to assess the impact of their personal and investment profile on the type of investor category they belong to, and the extent of influence on their Earned Returns on Investment. The research study further extends to examine the level or intensity of biasness under each category of investors.

The investment decisions were found to vary from one person to the other based on their risk potential, which affects their returns to a large extent. The effect of loss is much stronger than the effect of a gain in an investment. Several decisions have been extensively decisive in certain critical situations in the stock market, when it becomes fatal resulting in unbearable losses, for some investors, who decide to flee from the market. Hence, this study intended to explore on the decision biases and to suggest on the necessity of the improvisation of the behavioral characteristics of investors in taking decisions, during certain crucial occasions.

Further analysis on the behavioral biases of investors based on the level of risk-taking capacity of investors of the Indian stock market may reveal some interesting relationship between the types of investors and the behavioral biases and their earned return.

Scope and Limitations of the Study

Behavioral finance is envisioning a new branch of capital market analysis, covering psychology and economics. The encounter between 'understanding' (theory) and 'experience' (practice) proved to be extremely productive, confirming Kant's statement that "understanding without experience remains as empty as experience without understanding is blind". Most of the theoretical aspects which had been intuitively grasped, had sublimate to become clear and transparent. This research in the area of Behavioral Finance, is subject to an ongoing change with several new attributes in behavior of investors but which ultimately arise from the original principles. This is an attempt where it is highly difficult to examine all the aspects of human behavior, due to the varying economical and financial conditions, and for which reason only the most imperative behavioral biases could be analyzed in toto.

In any behavioral research it is the ambiguity that often arises when respondents are exposed to a few critical situations, for them to make decisions on financial judgments. Given the nature of behavioral finance, the limitations are inherent to all such studies. These limitations do not detract the value of the study, rather, they should be taken to point out the precautions to be observed in understanding and comparing the results. Moreover the behavior of human, especially relating to financial decisions, seems to be more erratic, and the consistency in such decisions hardly to be sustained.

The behavioral factors stem from literature on Western Studies. The identification of behavioral traits that has guided an important part of the present research is based on certain ontological assumptions which do not lend themselves to scientific verification.

The methodology for identification, classifying and measuring of several behavioral factors and patterns were only one of the different possibilities and is not a perfect one. As such, in an exploratory study on decision-making biases, these weaknesses are unavoidable and one has to use the findings with one's own maturity and understanding and insight to arrive at practical solutions or even explanations of reality.

Chapter Scheme

Chapter I : Introduction

This chapter presents the background and the problem of the study, outlines the importance, sets out the objectives, and presents the research methodology adopted, and indicates the scope and limitations of the study.

Chapter II : Capital Market Behavior in India

The second chapter discusses the mechanics of stock market operations and its functional aspects. It highlights the implications of the global scenario especially the US economy on the Indian Capital Market. It also projects the growth of the stock market in India after post- liberalization, and the roller coaster ride of sensex until December 2008.

Chapter III : Behavioral Finance – A Conceptual Analysis and Review of Research Studies

The third chapter contains three parts. The first part discusses about the Behavioral finance and stock market anomalies in general. The second part provides a brief overview about the EMH (Efficient Market Hypothesis) theory and the third part presents the conceptual and theoretical aspects with a brief Review of Literature of the study.

Chapter IV : Personal Factors and Investment Profile of Investors

This chapter provides an analysis on the demographic variables and personal interests relating to the Behavioral category of the investors based on their intensity of risk taken. These factors explains its relationship with the investor type they belong to.

Chapter V : Heuristic Behavioral Factors of Investors

This chapter provides an analysis to identify the various dominating factors manifesting judgmental errors, which are termed as cognitive biases or Heuristics, influencing the investment decisions considered as irrational affecting their Earned Returns.

Chapter VI : Personal Factors, Investment Profile and Return on Investments

This chapter analyses the association between personal factors and the return on Investment; Investment Profile of investors and the Return on Investment.

Chapter VII : Types of Investors and Heuristic Biases

The types of investors were classified according to the level of risk-taking capacity. These three categories of investors possess the judgmental biases at varied levels either low or moderate or high level. This chapter associates the relationship of the level of biasness in each type of investor.

Chapter VIII : Summary and Conclusion

An overall review of the findings of the study has been presented in this chapter from the analysis of the preceding chapters. The findings projects the implications of the Heuristics on the Behavioral Types of investors and its impact on their Average Earned Return. A few directions for future research is also suggested.

Footnotes

1. A recent example in January 2008, sensex reaching an all time high of 21000 followed by a downward steep fall in November 2008 to a low of 8000 in a period of 10 months.
2. 'Behaviour' for the purpose of this study is taken to mean the investment decisions of investors in stock market with reference to their risk potential.

3. 'Returns' for the purpose of this study include the amount invested in purchasing stock securities plus capital appreciation and income earned emerging from their portfolio investment .

* Source: Bangalore Directory for Members, from the website of bangalore stockexchange.com. (Appendix- 1)

2

Capital Market Behavior in India

Understanding the concepts and terminologies applied in capital Market Analysis and the behavior of stock markets reflected through price variations of the stocks and indices of stock exchanges in India, and tracing the reasons for volatile behavior of stock market are necessary prelude to gain deeper knowledge on Behavioral Finance. Moreover, any attempt to study the heuristic behavioral factors of investors without understanding and analyzing the stock market behavior is a futile exercise. Therefore an attempt is made in this chapter to highlight these issues.

Financial Market Mechanism

A *Financial market* is a mechanism that allows people to easily buy and sell (trade) financial securities (such as stocks and bonds), commodities (such as precious metals or agricultural goods), and other fungible items of value at low transaction costs and at prices that reflect the efficient-market hypothesis.

In finance, financial markets facilitate in ;

- The raising of capital (in the capital markets);
- The transfer of risk (in the derivatives markets);
- International trade (in the currency markets)

and are used to match those who *want* capital to those who *have* it.

The *Capital market* is the market for securities, where companies and governments can raise long term funds. The capital markets consist of *primary* markets and *secondary* markets. The primary market is where new stock and bonds issues are sold (underwritten) to investors. The secondary markets are where existing securities are sold and bought from one investor or speculator to another, usually on an exchange (eg.- National Stock Exchange; Bombay Stock Exchange).

Capital markets consists of (i) *Stock markets,* which provide financing through the issuance of shares or common stock, and enable the subsequent trading thereof and (ii) *Bond markets,* which provide financing through the issuance of bonds, and enable the subsequent trading thereof. (iii) *Commodity markets,* which facilitate the trading of commodities (iv) *Money markets,* which provide short term debt financing and investment (v) *Derivatives markets,* which provide instruments for the management of financial risk. (vi) *Futures markets,* which provide standardized forward contracts for trading products at some future date. (vii) *Insurance markets,* which facilitate the redistribution of various risks. (viii) *Foreign exchange markets,* which facilitate the trading of foreign exchange.

Primary market constitute new issue of shares such as;

(i) *IPOs and FPOs-* (Initial Public Offering and Follow-on Public offering) – IPO refers to the selling of shares by a private company to the public for the first time. Initial Public Offering is a source of funds raised from the primary market. All subsequent public offerings are known as Follow-on Public Offerings or Secondary Market Offerings.

(ii) *Book Building-* Book building is a process of price discovery used in Initial Public Offering. As per SEBI guidelines, Book Building is defined as "a process undertaken by which a demand for the securities proposed to be issued by a body corporate is elicited and built-up and the price for such securities is assessed for the determination of the quantum of such securities to be issued by means of a notice, circular, advertisement, document or information memoranda or offer document". Investors bid at different prices which may be equal to or more than the floor price and the issue price of shares is determined at the end of the bidding period.

(iii) *Fixed Price Issue-* In a book building issue, there is a price band where in the lower price is the floor price and the higher price is the ceiling price. Investors may bid at the floor price or higher than the floor price. And based upon this process the issue of price is determined. Whereas in fixed price issue, there is no price band and therefore investors have to apply at only one price. In a Book Building issue, the demand can be seen on a daily basis as the bids are received and the book is built, whereas, in a Fixed Price issue, demand can be ascertained only at the close of the issue.

Secondary market pertains to buying and selling of existing securities through an intermediary (eg.stock exchange). A *stock exchange* or *securities exchange* or *bourse* (in Europe) is a corporation or mutual organisation which provides "trading" facilities for stock brokers and traders, to trade stocks and other securities. Stock exchanges also provide facilities for the issue and redemption of securities as well as other financial instruments and capital events including the payment of income and dividends. Under a Secondary Market Offering of shares to raise money or conversion of reserves to inflate capital, a company can opt for a *rights issue* and *bonus issue.*

(i) *Rights Issue-* Shares issued by the company to the existing shareholders who have the privilege to buy a specified number of new shares from the firm at a specified price within a specified time. A rights issue is offered to all existing shareholders individually and may be rejected, accepted in full or accepted in part. Rights are often transferable, allowing the holder to sell them on the open market.

(ii) *Bonus Issue-* Shares issued to the existing shareholders by converting free reserves or share premium account to equity capital without taking any consideration from investors. Bonus shares do not directly affect a company's performance.

The effective functioning of capital market operations are driven by the '*Financial Market Participants*', whose contribution has brought tremendous changes and strategic development in volumes, technology and regulations. Some of the pertinent financial market participants are;

(i) *Retail Investor*- An *investor* makes an Investment by regularly purchasing equity or debt securities for financial gain. A retail investor is an individual investor possessing shares of a given security, on his own or on behalf of his client as a stock broker.

(ii) *A Stockbroker or Brokerage House*- An entity affiliated to a stock market who bridges the gap between an investor and a stock market to buy or sell stocks and shares.

(iii) *Speculator*- Speculators in an asset have no intention to have long term exposure on the asset. It involves the buying, holding, selling, and short-selling of stocks, bonds, commodities, currencies, collectibles, real estate, derivatives or any valuable financial instrument to profit from fluctuations in its price as opposed to buying it for long term use or for earning income.

(iv) *Institutional Investor*- An institutional investor is an investor, such as a bank, insurance company, retirement fund, hedge fund, or mutual fund, that is financially sophisticated and makes large investments, often held in very large portfolios of investments.

(v) *FIIs (Foreign Institutional Investors)*- An investor or investment fund that is from or registered in a country outside of the one in which it is currently investing. Institutional investors include hedge funds, insurance companies, pension funds and mutual funds. International institutional investors must register with the Securities and Exchange Board of India to participate in the market. One of the major market regulations pertaining to FIIs involves placing limits on FII ownership in Indian companies. Termed as

Elephants are large institutions that have the funds to make high volumes trades. Due to the large volumes of stock that elephants deal in, any investment decisions that they make will have a large influence on the price of the underlying financial asset. If an elephant steps into the pool (buys into a position), the water level (stock price) increases; if the elephant gets out of the pool (sells a position), the water level (stock price) decreases. In comparison to the elephant's influence on stock prices, the effect of an individual investor is more like that of a mouse.

Barometer of Stock Movement – 'Index' a Measure of Performance

Stock Market Index– is a statistical measure of changes in the stock market ie., a measure of performance of underlying stocks. Changes in the index reflects changes in the value of stocks. An index *[Sensitivity index of 30 stocks (ie., sensex of BSE) and National Stock Exchange Index of 50 stocks (ie., Nifty of NSE)]* represents a portfolio of securities traded on the market that reflects the market as a whole. It is a convenient way to determine if the market is on the way up or down.

Sensex is calculated on the basis of Free-Float market capitalization.. Market capitalization (mid-cap, small-cap and large-cap) is the worth of the company in terms of its shares (current price multiplied by the number of shares issued by the company), whereas the float shares are open market shares (excluding promoters and other long term holdings). The product of free-float factor and 'market cap' of that company gives free-float market capitalization. Sensex, compiled in 1986, with its 30 component stocks representing large and financially sound companies, across 12 major sectors are chosen based on certain stringent criteria such as the scrip to be listed for atleast three months at BSE, traded everyday during this period and the three months average free-float market cap should be atleast 0.5% of the index, backed with good track record inclusive of dividend payments.

The Ups and Lows of Sensex from 1992 to 2008

The year 2008 was the worst year for investments. The price fall in all asset classes was steep around 65 to 75 percent. None of the scrips in this period yielded any reasonable returns except for those investors who went short. Even a novice having a foresight made money by short selling. During the period 1992-93, sensex lost 56 % from a high of 4546 to touch a low of 1980. The period 2000-01 experienced a dip of 58% from a high of 6150 to a low of 2594 points and now in 2008 (January to December) there has been a fall of 60% from the peak value. Predictions of economic malaise to persist upto April 2009, termed as a Fibonacci correction of the rise from September 2001 to January 2008. Sensex on 5th January 2009, was back at 10000 level, boosted by the policy measures and stimulus packages announced on the weekend of December 2008.

Evolution and Services of Stock Exchanges in India

Since 1991, a number of measures have been introduced for improving share trading and delivery mechanisms and investor protection ranging from more periodic disclosures, takeover regulations, insider trading rules, corporate governance code, etc. by the Securities and Exchange Board of India (SEBI), the market regulator. Out of the 23 stock exchanges in India, the most prominent in terms of Volumes and listed companies are the *NSE* (National Stock Exchange and the *BSE* (Bombay Stock Exchange).

BSE (Bombay Stock Exchange)

BSE's pivotal and pre-eminent role in the development of the Indian capital market is widely recognized. It migrated from the open outcry system to an online screen-based order driven trading system in 1995. BSE was established as "The Native Share & Stock Brokers' Association" in 1875, is the oldest stock exchange in Asia . BSE is now a corporatised and demutualised entity having two of world's best exchanges, Deutsche Börse and Singapore Exchange, as its strategic partners. It is the world's number 1 exchange in terms of the number of listed companies and the world's 5th in transaction numbers.

Services of BSE

(i) *The BSE On-line Trading (BOLT):* BSE On-line Trading (BOLT) facilitates on-line screen based trading in securities.

(ii) *Surveillance:* BSE's On-Line Surveillance System (BOSS) monitors on a real-time basis the price movements, volume positions and members' positions and real-time measurement of default risk, market reconstruction and generation of cross market alerts.

(iii) *BSEWEBX.com:* In February 2001, BSE introduced the world's first centralized exchange-based Internet trading system, BSEWEBX.com. to enable investors anywhere in the world to trade on the BSE platform.

(iv) *'BSE Broadcast'* - a unique ticker-cum-screen which enables information dissemination to the common man on the street.

(v) *BSE Index-* SENSEX, is India's first stock market index that enjoys an iconic stature. Apart from the SENSEX, BSE offers 21 indices, including 12 sectoral indices.

NSE (National Stock Exchange)

The need for setting up the National Stock Exchange arose from concerns of investors with the state of existing trading and settlement facilities. NSE was incorporated in 1992. Investors in many areas of the country did not have the same access and opportunity to trade as their counterparts in Mumbai or the main metros. The NSE network has been designed to provide equal access to investors from anywhere in India and to be responsive to their needs. This translates into a single dynamic market across the country with greatly enhanced liquidity, unparalleled transparency and safety. Investors located in remote corners of the country are now able to transact with investors across the country with ease and efficiency.

Trading and Risk Management Mechanism of NSE

(i) *Electronic Trading-* NSE introduced for the first time in India fully screen based trading, thereby eliminating the need for physical trading floors. The brokers can now trade from their offices wherever they are located. They are connected to the Exchange from their workstations to the central computer located at the Exchange via. Satellite using VSATs (Very Small Aperture Terminals).

(ii) *NSE Index-* As of now, more than 1400 companies are available for trading on the NSE. The N S E-50 Index is a market capitalization weighted index comprising 50 scientifically selected stocks having the highest liquidity and largest market capitalization. The companies are selected based on their paid-up capital, market capitalization, dividend payment and a good track record. The criterion is meant to ensure that only companies that meet certain standards are listed. This list is reviewed at periodic intervals.

(iii) *Price-time Priority -* The system arranges all orders in the priority of price and within price by time.

(iv) *Matching Order System-* The NSE trading system matches orders in such a way that the order is executed at the best possible price available on the system.

(v) *Derivatives Trading-* NSE commenced trading in *Index Futures* on June 2000, *Index options* in June 2001, *Stock options* in July 2001 and *Stock Futures* in November 2001. It has recently launched *Currency derivatives* in August 2008.

Table 1 Discloses the Growth History of NSE from 1995 to 2008.

Table 1
Growth History of NSE (1995-2008)

Year	*No.of Companies listed*	*No. of Trades (lakh)*	*Turnover (Rs.cr)*	*Market Capitalisation (Rs.cr)*	*% Change*
1994 - 95	135	3	1805	363,350	-
1995 – 96	422	66	67287	401,415	10.5
1996 – 97	550	264	294,503	419,367	4.5
1997 – 98	612	381	370,193	481,503	14.8
1998 – 99	648	546	414,474	491,175	2.0
1999 - 2000	720	984	839,052	1020,426	107.8
2000 – 01	785	1676	1339,510	657,847	-35.5
2001 – 02	793	1753	513,167	636,861	-3.2

Contd.

Year	*No.of Companies listed*	*No. of Trades (lakh)*	*Turnover (Rs.cr)*	*Market Capitalisation (Rs.cr)*	*% Change*
2002 – 03	818	2398	617,989	537,133	-15.7
2003 – 04	909	3780	1099,535	1120,976	108.7
2004 – 05	970	4510	1140,071	1585,585	41.4
2005 – 06	1069	6088	1569,556	2813,201	77.4
2006 – 07	1228	7846	1945,285	3367,350	19.7
2007 - 08	1381	11727	3551,038	4858,122	44.3

Source: nse-india.com

Table No. 1, shows a decline in the market capitalisation during the years 2000-'01, 2001-'02, 2002-'03 and again in 2006-'07. The number of companies listed and Number of trades has a substantial increase over the period from 1994 to 2008. The turnover and growth of Market capitalisation is depicted in Fig. 1.

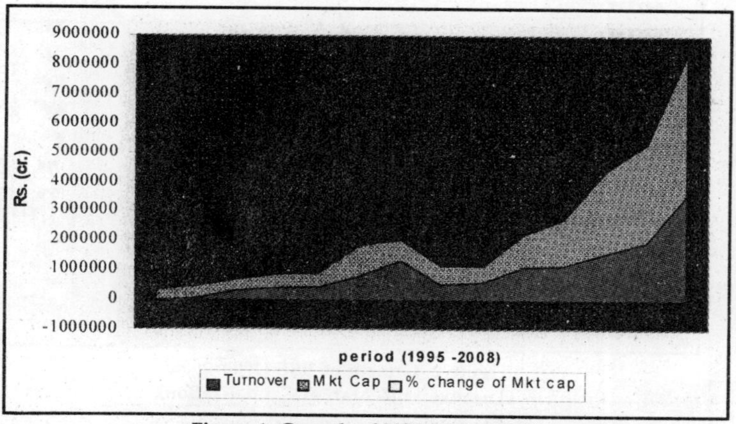

Figure 1: Growth of NSE (1995 -2008)
(Turnover and Market Capitalization)

The growth history of BSE between 2000 and 2008 is shown in Table 2 and the movement is exposed in the Fig. No. 2.

A cursory look at Table 2 reveals a decline in the market capitalisation during the years 2000-'01 and 2001-'02, and had substantially increased during the period 2003- '04. There has been a 97.8% increase in market capitalisation and 91.2% increase of turnover during the period 2006-07.

Table 2
Growth History of BSE (2000–2008)

Year	*No. of Companies Listed*	*No. of Scrips Listed*	*No. of Trades ('000s)*	*Turnover (Rs.cr)*	*Market Capitalisation (Rs.cr)*	*% Change*
1999 - 2000	5863	7118	8091.78	78447.56	803353	0
2000 – 01	5937	9451	14402.73	99198.69	691162	-14.0
2001 – 02	5795	6365	12046.83	30032.96	532328	-23.0
2002 – 03	5650	7279	12310.55	30581.59	628197	18.0
2003 – 04	5644	7368	179594.24	54815.54	1273361	102.7
2004 – 05	4730	6942	168073.15	50225.66	1685989	32.4
2005 – 06	4763	7236	187382.23	77356.08	2489386	47.7
2006 – 07	4796	7500	30632.57	85512.18	3624357	45.6
2007 - 08	4887	7706	385671.29	163515.56	7169985	97.8

Source: bseindia.com

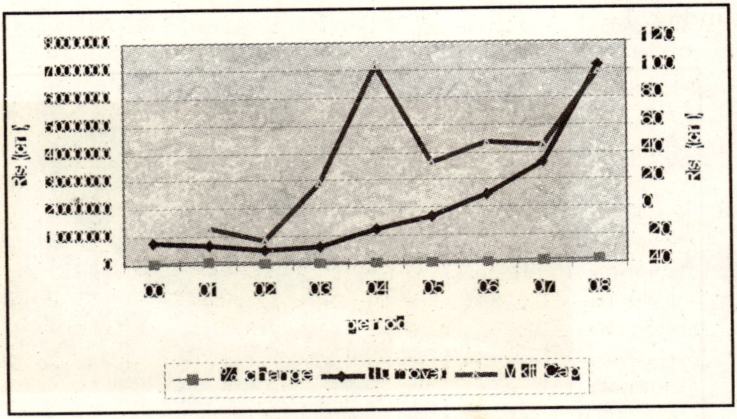

Figure 2: Growth of BSE (2000–2008)
(Turnover and Market Capitalization)

Table No. 3 shows the Movement of Sensex in BSE for the period 2005 to 2008.

The sensex started to decline from 12th January 2008 onwards. From Table No. 3, it is observed a huge decline of 15% at the end of January 2008. From the peak of sensex at 21206 a tremendous fall is observed during the end of the year 2008. A fall of 19% on 31st March 2008, 29% fall as on 31st July 2008 and a 52% fall as on 31st December 2008 from the sensex high as on 11th January 2008. The reasons behind the fall in sensex during different periods has been examined in the succeeding pages of this chapter.

Table 3
Monthwise Index Movement of BSE Sensex
(Jan. 2005 to Dec. 2008)

Month & Year	*Sensex High*	*% Change*	*Month & Year*	*Sensex High*	*% Change*
31-Jan-05	6696.31	0	31-Jan-07	14325.92	2.1
28-Feb-05	6721.08	0.4	28-Feb-07	14723.88	2.8
31-Mar-05	6954.86	3.5	30-Mar-07	13386.95	-9.1
29-Apr-05	6649.42	-4.4	30-Apr-07	14383.72	7.4
31-May-05	6772.74	1.9	31-May-07	14576.37	1.3
30-Jun-05	7228.21	6.7	29-Jun-07	14683.36	0.7
29-Jul-05	7708.59	6.6	30-Jul-07	15868.85	8.1
31-Aug-05	7921.39	2.8	31-Aug-07	15542.40	-2.1
30-Sep-05	8722.17	10.1	28-Sep-07	17361.47	11.7
31-Oct-05	8821.84	1.1	31-Oct-07	20238.16	16.6
30-Nov-05	9033.99	2.4	30-Nov-07	20204.21	-0.2
30-Dec-05	9442.98	4.5	31-Dec-07	20498.11	1.5
2-Jan-06	9457.09	0.1	1-Jan-08	20394.89	-0.5
9-Jan-06	9689.68	2.5	11-Jan-08	21206.77	4.0
31-Jan-06	9939.55	2.6	31-Jan-08	18008.71	-15.1
28-Feb-06	10422.65	4.9	29-Feb-08	18894.34	4.9
31-Mar-06	11356.95	9.0	31-Mar-08	17227.56	-8.8
29-Apr-06	12102	6.6	30-Apr-08	17480.74	1.5
31-May-06	12671.11	4.7	30-May-08	17735.70	1.5
30-Jun-06	10626.84	-16.1	30-Jun-08	16632.72	-6.2
31-Jul-06	10940.45	3.0	31-Jul-08	15130.09	-9.0
31-Aug-06	11794.43	7.8	29-Aug-08	15579.78	3.0
29-Sep-06	12485.17	5.9	30-Sep-08	15107.01	-3.0
31-Oct-06	13075.85	4.7	31-Oct-08	13203.86	-12.6
30-Nov-06	13799.08	5.5	28-Nov-08	10945.41	-17.1
29-Dec-06	14035.30	1.7	31-Dec-08	10188.54	-6.9

Source: bseindia.com

Figure 3 shows the Monthwise movement of Index for a period of four years from 2005 to 2008.

Month wise Index movement of Nifty for a period from 2005 to 2008 is shown in Table No. 4 along with the percentage change from the previous months.

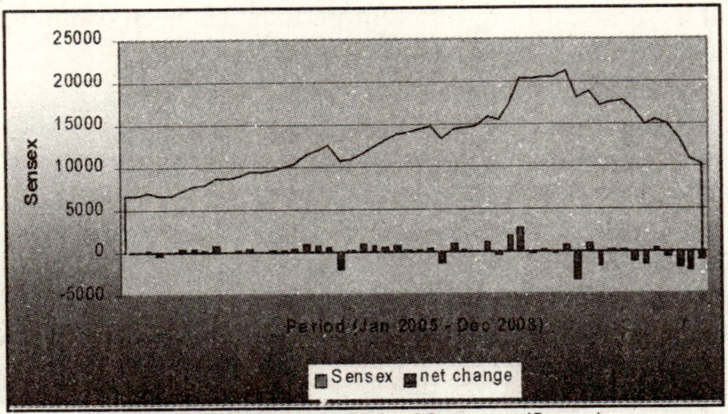

Figure 3: Month-wise Index Movement (Sensex) (Jan. 2005 to Dec. 2008)

Table 4
Month-wise Index Movement of Nifty
(Jan. 2005 to Dec. 2008)

Month & Year	*Nifty High*	*% Change*	*Month & Year*	*Nifty High*	*% Change*
31-Jan-05	2060.40	0	31-Jan-07	4137.85	3.7
28-Feb-05	2106.20	2.22	28-Feb-07	3893.40	-5.9
31-Mar-05	2043.60	-2.97	30-Mar-07	3832.20	-1.6
29-Apr-05	1943.20	-4.91	30-Apr-07	4096.90	6.9
31-May-05	2091.75	7.64	31-May-07	4306.75	5.1
30-Jun-05	2226.15	6.43	29-Jun-07	4321.35	0.3
29-Jul-05	2332.55	4.78	30-Jul-07	4493.05	4.0
31-Aug-05	2387.00	2.33	31-Aug-07	4471.30	-0.5
30-Sep-05	2623.05	9.89	28-Sep-07	5055.80	13.1
31-Oct-05	2373.40	-9.52	31-Oct-07	5952.25	17.7
30-Nov-05	2727.05	14.90	30-Nov-07	5782.55	-2.9
30-Dec-05	2845.55	4.35	31-Dec-07	6167.75	6.7
2-Jan-06	2849.45	0.14	1-Jan-08	6165.35	0.0
9-Jan-06	2927.25	2.73	11-Jan-08	6357.10	3.1
31-Jan-06	3005.10	2.66	31-Jan-08	5251.65	-17.4
28-Feb-06	3090.30	2.84	29-Feb-08	5290.80	0.7
31-Mar-06	3425.45	10.85	31-Mar-08	4947.00	-6.5
29-Apr-06	3565.75	4.10	30-Apr-08	5230.75	5.7
31-May-06	3181.95	-10.76	30-May-08	4908.85	-6.2
30-Jun-06	3134.15	-1.50	30-Jun-08	4163.00	-15.2
31-Jul-06	3179.70	1.45	31-Jul-08	4342.00	4.3
31-Aug-06	3452.30	8.57	29-Aug-08	4368.80	0.6

Contd.

Month & Year	*Nifty High*	*% Change*	*Month & Year*	*Nifty High*	*% Change*
29-Sep-06	3599.80	4.27	30-Sep-08	3966.85	-9.2
31-Oct-06	3782.85	5.09	31-Oct-08	2921.35	-26.4
30-Nov-06	3973.00	5.03	28-Nov-08	2779.00	-4.9
29-Dec-06	3991.60	0.47	31-Dec-08	3002.65	8.0

Source: nse-india.com

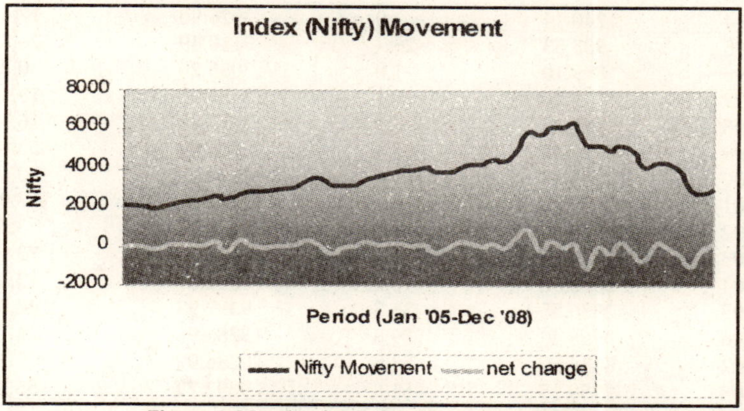

Figure 4: Month-wise Index Movement of Nifty (Jan. 2005 to Dec. 2008)

As observed in sensex levels, the Nifty also followed a similar pattern as exhibited in Table 4. The Nifty high was observed on 11th January 2008 at 6357 and the decline compared to this level was found to be 17% as at the end of the month, 28% as on 31st March, 2008 ; 53% as on 30th June 2008; 128% as on 28th November 2008 and 112% as at the end of the year 2008. The reasons due to increase and decrease of Nifty has been discussed in the succeeding pages of this chapter. The monthwise index movement of Nifty is shown in Fig.4

The year wise index movement of both Nifty and Sensex for a period of 18 years from 1991 to 2008 has been shown in Table No. 5 with the percentage change of increase or decrease of the indices.

The graphical presentation of the yearwise index movement of Nifty and sensex alongwith the percentage change year wise is depicted in Fig. 5

Table 5
Year -wise Index (Nifty and Sensex) Movement
(1991 to 2008)

Year	*Nifty Close*	*% Change*	*Sensex Close*	*% Change*
1991	-	-	1908.85	0
1992	-	-	2615.37	37.0
1993	-	-	3346.06	27.9
1994	1240.14	0	3926.90	17.4
1995	908.53	-26.7	3110.49	-20.8
1996	899.10	-1.0	3085.20	-0.8
1997	1079.40	20.1	3658.98	18.6
1998	884.25	-18.1	3055.41	-16.5
1999	1480.45	67.4	5005.82	63.8
2000	1263.55	-14.7	3972.12	-20.6
2001	1059.05	-16.2	3262.33	-17.9
2002	1093.50	3.3	3377.28	3.5
2003	1879.75	71.9	5838.96	72.9
2004	2080.50	10.7	6602.69	13.1
2005	2836.55	36.3	9397.93	42.3
2006	3966.40	39.8	13786.91	46.7
2007	6138.60	54.8	20286.99	47.1
2008	2959.15	-51.8	9092.72	-55.2

Source: nse-india.com; bseindia

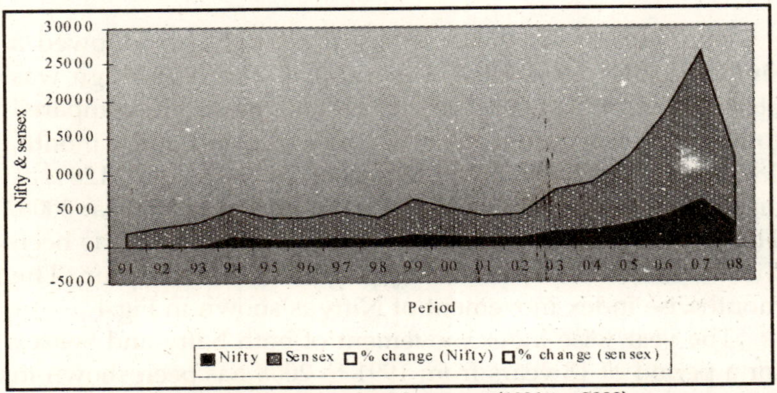

Figure 5: Year-wise Index Movement (1991 to 2008)

The percentage change of Nifty and Sensex is the percentage increase or decrease of the current year from the previous year. In the year 1999, there has been an increase of Nifty by 67.4%, in the year 2003 an increase of 71.9% and in the year 2007 an increase of 54.8%. The table shows a fall in

Nifty by 54.8% in the year 2008. Similarly the Sensex shows 63.8% increase in the year 1999, 72.9% increase in the year 2003 and 47% increase in the year 2007. It exhibits a 55% fall of Sensex in the year 2008. Figure 5 represents the yearwise index movement of Nifty and Sensex.

Sensex Drive due to Positive and Negative Sentiments–Market Analysis on the Bull Run and Bear Phase

"Bull markets are born on pessimism, grow on skepticism, mature on optimism, and die on euphoria. The time of maximum pessimism is the best time to buy, and the time of maximum optimism is the best time to sell," - Sir John Templeton[1] (founder of Franklin-Templeton). This holds true on a euphoria in the market and the lesson taught is 'buy when there`s blood in the streets'. The mayhem during the year 2008, was due to several reasons. Most particularly the global crisis, started from the sub-prime crisis in US, followed by the bankruptcy of top banks of US forcing a recession in the US economy and its global implications. The Indian history of slumps and growth in Capital Market has been tracked from the year 1991(post globalisation) to 2008 as given in Table 1, 2 and 3.

1991 - 1992 : In 1991, a group of stockbrokers, headed by key trader 'Big Bull' Harshad Mehta artificially jacked up prices of worthless securities to rake in Rs 5,000 crore (Rs 50 billion). The Sensex came tumbling down after the scam story broke out on April 23, 1992. Fortunes were lost overnight. As a result, the ambit of the Securities Exchange Board of India, the stock exchanges and regulatory financial institutions was widened.

1994-96 : From 1994 to 1996, the markets did get enormous changes to the technology of trading, but the basic structure of the market was unchanged. There was still trading over an "account period" of a week, followed by settlement the next week. Even this once-a-week settlement was optional because the markets were still running badla. The last nail in the coffin was the unseemly spectacle of SEBI dragging its feet from 1996 onwards on the moving from badla to derivatives. This became an inevitable setting for disaster, especially in combination with a deliberate intent to fraud on the part of some players[2].

1998 - 1999 : The capital market witnessed a drop in market during this period due to US64 which reported a large drop in its NAV in 1998, for which the Ministry of Finance put up roughly Rs.1800 crore of public money.

1999 – 2001 : Over the period of 1999 to early 2001, the rise and subsequent fall in the market values would have been less exacerbated if there was a clear separation of the markets for those who wanted to buy the share and those who wanted to take a forward position on the share.

2000 -2001 – Nearly a decade later, on February 28 2001, the Bombay Stock Exchange index rose initially but thereafter crashed. Nearly 700 points were lost in eight trading sessions leading to erosion in market capitalisation of Rs 146,000 crore (Rs 1,460 billion). This erratic behaviour was once again traced to a handful of brokers, wishing to trap a leading 'bull', Ketan Parekh, who had manipulated prices of shares of a few select companies in information technology, communication and entertainment sector[3].

Ketan Parekh and his associates, who were instrumental in the stock scam of 1999-2001, was accused for a criminal conspiracy to siphon off Rs 47.7 crore (Rs 477 million), misappropriation of funds and cheating. The modus operandi of the scam was that, huge amounts of money was transferred from Banglore-based Canbank Financial Services (Canfina), a subsidiary of Canara Bank to Mumbai-based Canbank Mutual Fund (CBMF) (another subsidiary of Canara Bank) between October 1991 to January 1992. This was purportedly for the purchase of government securities for Canfina, but in reality the money were transferred to the accounts of Parekh, Dalal and other three stock brokers, namely S K Jhaveri, Pallav Seth and Navinchandra Parekh (Ketan's uncle).The brokers used the money to the tune of Rs 47.7 crore for investing in stock market. At the end of the financial year, the money was returned to Canfina.

The effect of which, SEBI banned them for a total of 14 years effective from December 12, 2003. The investigations revealed that Ketan V. Parekh and 17 other entities who were directly or indirectly associated to him were involved in the manipulation of around eight scrips namely Himachal Futuristic Communications, Zee Telefilms, Adani Exports, Global Tele-Systems, Ranbaxy Laboratories, Shri Adhikari Brothers Television Network, Shonkh Technologies International, Padmini Technologies and Aftek Infosys. The events of September 11, 2001, too shook markets across the globe. The main financial market response was a flight where investors' appetite for risks fell. All major stock markets experienced rapid, sharp price declines in the immediate aftermath of the event.

On 2nd July 2001, two important changes took place that ultimately made it decisively different from the point of view of ease to manipulate: first, all exchanges moved to rolling settlement for the largest stocks in the country. Second, SEBI banned badla in the market for the second time in the reforms process, and exchanges moved more decisively into trading derivatives by starting trading in options.

2003 – 2007 : India had a dream run of five years during 2003-07 as the GDP growth averaged nearly 9 per cent annually for five years, the best ever five year 'Big Bull' run made everyone that there will always be sunshine. Investors tended to ignore warning signs and just brushed them aside as an aberration. On May 15, 2006 Sensex lost 462.91 points on the global meltdown of metal prices. SENSEX which reached a life-time high upto 18000, crashed 1744 points, on 17th August, 2007, after SEBI put up its suggestion on the p-Notes (Participatory Notes) said be behind the huge surge in foreign inflows, which caused the latest market rally. Sensex on October,2007 was 19051, which was a stupendous and a mountainous rise from 18000 to 19000 in as little as 4 days to surmount and this was associated with a net FII inflows around \$9.5 billion (\$7.2 billion invested in September 2007 alone). Historically such periods of exuberance have been followed by what is called a "Graveyard market", which was a steep decline, of 50 to 60% , starting from January 2008 onwards.

2008 - 2009 : The global financial crisis started off with the Sub-prime crisis, when the US housing bubble burst and borrowers started defaulting on their mortgage payments, and the value of the mortgage securities fell precipitously. What started as a crisis in some specific parts of the US later became a worldwide financial crisis. The bankruptcy of *Lehman Brothers* was the largest bankruptcy filing in U.S. history on September 15, 2008 with Lehman holding over $600 billion in assets, on which day the Dow Jones closed down just over 500 points. In 2008, Lehman faced an unprecedented loss due to the continuing subprime mortgage crisis. Then came the absorption of Merrill Lynch bought for $50 billion by Bank of America, the unparalleled government rescue of giant insurer American International Group (AIG) by funding $85bn (€59bn, £47bn) of taxpayers' money, Bear Stearns being acquired by JPMorgan Chase in March 2008, and the takeover of mortgage-finance giants Fannie Mae and Freddie Mac. The credit crisis of Wachovia, Washington Mutual (WaMu), Morgan Stanley and Goldman Sachs had added additional stress to find merger partners by the US Federal Reserve, which did not want to see some more spectacular collapses at Wall Street. The Satyam computers scam , brought the sensex down by 746 points on January 7, 2009.

Derivatives - Products and Growth in India

During the 1980s and 1990s, a major growth sector in financial markets is the trade in so called *derivative products*, or derivatives for short. In the financial markets, stock prices, bond prices, currency rates, interest rates and dividends go up and down, creating *risk.* Derivative products are financial products which are used to *control* risk or paradoxically *exploit* risk. *Derivatives* are financial contracts, or financial instruments, whose values are derived from the value of an *underlying asset* (e.g., commodities, equities (stocks), residential mortgages, commercial real estate, loans, bonds), an index (e.g., interest rates, exchange rates, stock market indices, consumer price index (CPI), or other derivatives (e.g., weather conditions, etc). Credit derivatives are based on loans, bonds or other forms of credit. Derivatives can be used to mitigate the risk of economic loss arising from changes in the value of the underlying, known as *hedging.*

The main types of derivatives are: *Forwards* (which if traded on an exchange are known as *Futures*); *options*; and *swaps*.

Future is a contract between a buyer and a seller, which binds the buyer to purchase and the seller to sell the stock or commodity at a future date at a fixed price. An *option* on the other hand is the privilege sold by one party to another that offers the buyer the right, but not the obligation, to buy (call) or sell (put) a security at an agreed-upon price during a certain period of time or on a specific date. A *swap* is a derivative in which two counterparties agree to exchange one stream of cash flows against another stream (eg. Interest rate swap , currency swap etc.,). An *Interest rate swap.* is the exchange of a fixed rate loan to a floating rate loan. The life of the swap can range from 2 years to over 15 years. The reason for this exchange is to take benefit from comparative advantage. Some companies may have comparative advantage in fixed rate markets while other companies have a comparative advantage in floating rate markets. When companies want to borrow they look for cheap borrowing i.e. from the market where they have comparative advantage. However this may lead to a company borrowing fixed when it wants floating or borrowing floating when it wants fixed. This is where a swap comes in. A swap has the effect of transforming a fixed rate loan into a floating rate loan

Table 6
Business Growth in Derivatives Segment (Futures)

	Index Futures		*Stock Futures*		*Increase/decrease (Turnover) %*	
Year	*No. of Contracts*	*Turnover (Rs. Cr.)*	*No. of Contracts*	*Turnover (Rs. Cr.)*	*Index Futures*	*Stock Futures*
2000 - 01	90580	2365	-	-	-	-
2001 – 02	1025588	21483	1957856	51515	808	-
2002 – 03	2126763	43952	10676843	286533	105	456
2003 – 04	17191668	554446	32368842	1305939	1161	356
2004 – 05	21635449	772147	47043066	1484056	39	14
2005 – 06	58537886	1513755	80905493	2791697	96	88
2006 – 07	81487424	2539574	104955401	3830967	68	37
2007 - 08	156598579	3820667	203587952	7548563	50	97
2008 – Jan.09	156484642	2853615	171422782	2789329		

Source: nseindia.com (as on 10th Jan., 2009)
Note: Notional Turnover = (Strike Price + Premium) * Quantity

or vice versa. The *Currency Swap* involves exchanging principal and fixed rate interest payments on a loan in one currency for principal and fixed rate interest payments on an equal loan in another currency. Just like interest rate swaps, the currency swaps also are motivated by comparative advantage. A *commodity swap* is an agreement whereby a floating (or market or spot) price is exchanged for a fixed price over a specified period.

"Derivatives is a disastrous weapon of mass destruction", according to Warren Buffet which has been put in a different view as "Derivatives is a disastrous weapon of mass destruction, when used in a wrong sense at a wrong timing[4]"

Table No. 6 and 7 reveals the growth in Derivatives segment (Futures and Options) of Capital Market for the period 2000 to 2009 .

Table 6 and 7 reveals a tremendous growth in the Derivatives segment for the period from 2001 to 2008. It is found an increase of 808% of business growth in the turnover of Index futures from the year 2000 to 2002, a decline of 105% in the year 2003. There has been an increase of 1161% from 2003 to 2004 and a sharp decline to 39% in the year 2005 and 50% in the year 2008 in the growth of Index Futures. Similarly stock futures has shown a commendable growth in the year 2002 to 2004 and a sharp decline sustaining at 97% in the year 2008. The Average daily turnover was 327% and 379% during the period 2002 and 2004 after the introduction of options in the Indian Capital Market.

Impact of FIIs in India

India's exceptional growth story and its booming economy have made the country a favorite destination with Foreign Institutional Investors (FIIs). FIIs showed huge interest in 2007, pumping in the highest ever net investment of US$ 17.23 billion in the equity markets and were instrumental in the Bombay Stock Exchange (BSE) and National Stock Exchange (NSE) clocking record index levels of over 20,000 and 6,000, respectively. In fact, during the year, FIIs were net buyers in 10 out of 12 months, turning net sellers in the rest, primarily

Table 7

Business Growth In Derivatives Segment (Options)

Year	Index Options		Stock options		Total		
	No. of Contracts	Turnover (Rs. cr.)	No. of Contracts	Turnover (Rs. cr.)	No. of Contracts	Turnover (Rs. cr.)	Average Daily Turnover (Rs. cr.)
2000 - 01	-	-	-	-	-	-	-
2001 - 02	175900	3765	1037529	25163	4196873	101926	410
2002 - 03	442241	9246	3523062	100131	16768909	439862	1752
2003 - 04	1732414	52816	5583071	217207	56886776	2130610	8388
2004 - 05	3293558	121943	5045112	168836	77017185	2546982	10107
2005 - 06	12935116	338469	5240776	180253	157619271	4824174	19220
2006 - 07	25157438	791906	5283310	193795	216883573	7356242	29543
2007 - 08	55366038	1362111	9460631	359137	425013200	13090478	52153
2008 - 09	137949487	2672532	9190538	164586	47504744	8480063	46087

Source: nseindia.com (as on 10th Jan., 2009)

Note: The total Number of contracts and Turnover in 2003 - 04 includes Interest rate Futures also

to make up the losses on account of the sub-prime crisis in the US.

This surge in FII investment has led to the cumulative net investments by FIIs into Indian equities to total US$ 52.76 billion by the end of November 2008, since December 1993, when FIIs were allowed to enter India. As of November 28, 2008, 1581 FIIs and 4824 sub-accounts were registered with the Securities and Exchange Board of India (SEBI). Even during the market meltdown in 2008 the FIIs invested US$ 61.83 million in equities, on December 4, 2008, showing confidence in the Indian stock market.

Evaluation of Security – Models and Methods

Valuation is the process of determining the current worth of an asset or company. In general, the value of an asset is the price that a willing and able buyer pays to the willing and able seller. There are many techniques that can be used to determine value, some are subjective and others are objective. Valuation of a security guides the investor in picking the right stocks. There are several quantitative valuation models (Bond and Equity), such as Dividend Valuation Model, Gordon Growth model, Price Earnings Valuation model etc. taking into account the dividend earnings, future cash flow stream, and its selling price.

Investors who are risk averse, will choose to hold a portfolio of securities to take advantage of the benefits of Diversification. To decide whether or not to invest in a particular stock, they want to know how the stock will contribute to the risk and expected return of their portfolios. The standard deviation of an individual stock does not indicate how that stock will contribute to the risk and return of a diversified portfolio. Thus, another measure of risk is needed; a measure of a security's *systematic risk.* This measure is provided by the Capital Asset Pricing Model (CAPM).

CAPM (Capital Asset Pricing Model) : The Capital Asset Pricing Model (CAPM) provides an expression which relates the expected return on an asset to its systematic risk. An asset's total risk consists of both systematic and unsystematic risk. Systematic risk, which is also called market risk or undiversifiable risk, is the portion of an asset's risk that cannot be eliminated via diversification. The systematic risk indicates how including a particular asset in a diversified portfolio will contribute to the riskiness of the portfolio. Unsystematic risk, which is also called firm-specific or diversifiable risk, is the portion of an asset's total risk that can be eliminated by including the security as part of a diversifiable portfolio. The relationship of expected return and the systematic risk is referred as the *Security Market Line (SML)*[5] and the measure of systematic risk in the CAPM is called *Beta*.

Investing evokes a very wide variety of thoughts, emotions, and motivations. Conversations, the media, and popular literature contain significant unverified, biased, false, and sometimes simply ridiculous investment information. When such information is superficially plausible, it seems especially easy for erroneous beliefs to perpetuate and become part of widespread investment myths projecting bad investment ideas. For example, many individual investors believe that they have a good chance to consistently "beat-the-market." Such beliefs are played upon and are reinforced by others who stand to profit, that leads to poorly diversified portfolios with higher volatility and lower returns. Hence the investors need to realize that, they have to sort truth from fiction on their own without unbiased help from the industry. The methods used to analyze securities and make investment decisions fall into two very broad categories:

(i) Fundamental Analysis and/or

(ii) Technical Analysis.

Fundamental Analysis

Fundamental Analysis involves analyzing the characteristics of a company in order to estimate its value. Technical analysis takes a completely different approach; it does not attempt to measure a security's intrinsic value, but instead use charts and other tools to identify patterns of price movements in the market that can suggest future activity.

Fundamental Analysis measures the intrinsic value of a security by examining related economic, financial and other qualitative and quantitative factors. *Intrinsic value* is the present value of the expected future cash flows discounted at the decision-maker's required rate of return.

Fundamental analysts attempt to study everything that can affect the security's value, including macroeconomic factors (like the overall economy and industry conditions) and individually specific factors (like the financial condition and management of companies).

The end goal of performing fundamental analysis is to produce a value that an investor can compare with the security's current price in hopes of figuring out what sort of position to take with that security (underpriced = buy, overpriced = sell or short). This method of security analysis is considered to be the opposite of technical analysis. One of the most famous and successful users of fundamental analysis is the Oracle of Omaha, Warren Buffett, who has been well known for successfully employing fundamental analysis to pick securities. Some of the important observations about securities markets[6] are that:

- The aggregate market return consists of dividend gains plus capital gains or losses across all investors.
- Fundamentally, markets look forward. Participants attempt to peer into the murky and fundamentally unknowable spectrum of possible future events giving much importance for news rather than the stock fundamentals.
- Markets price securities on a risk-adjusted basis. Current securities prices are discounted versus their projected future values to reward certain kinds of risk taking.
- Current market prices reflect the expected risk and expected return.
- Current market prices tend to reflect fully all currently known information associated with a particular security. There may be a wide range in the interpretation of the importance of various information, and asset market values reflect the consensus across all investors.

- New information disseminates widely and very rapidly. Prices rapidly reflect new information, as supply and demand shifts quickly and market prices change accordingly.

When some investors "win," others must "lose" relative to the aggregate market return. Whether luck or skill determines who wins or loses and how one can tell the difference are pivotal questions in choosing investment strategies.

The components of fundamental analysis are *Economic Analysis; Industry Analysis* and *Company Analysis* which helps to interpret the correct value of securities in contrast with its market value.

Economic Analysis- Economic Indicators measure the economic health of the overall economy. Economic Analysis analyses the global economics, both international and national, such as *GDP* growth rates, *inflation, interest* rates, *exchange rates, productivity,* and energy prices. The economic indicators like CPI (consumer Price Index); (PPI) Producer Price Index; M2 (money supply) and GDP are commonly used by traders. This helps to narrow down the search in choosing the sector or the industry.

Industry Analysis- It helps to remain fully abreast of the trends in individual industries. It provides information relating to demand and supply; price levels; Investments made; Financial performance of each sector contributing to GDP; growth in sales; effect of competing products; foreign competition etc. The industry analysis guides in choosing the right industry for investment.

Company Analysis– is the analysis of individual companies based on their profits earned, turnover, income distributed, debt payments overdue, and accumulated reserves. The following measurement tools will help evaluate a company and determine the value of its stock such as Price-Earnings Ratio; Price-earnings to Growth ratio; Cash ratio; Debt-equity ratio; Earnings per share; Book to Market price ratio; Return on Investment; Dividend payout ratio etc.

Technical Analysis

Technical analysis is a method used to predict the future stock price movement using historic data. Technical analysis studies the *supply* and *demand* in a market in an attempt to determine what direction, or *trend,* will continue in the future. In other words, technical analysis attempts to understand the emotions in the market by studying the market itself, as opposed to its components. In this method, the financials of a company or not taken account, while deciding on buying or selling a stock. In technical analysis, the pattern of price and volumes of a stock traded are the key parameters. There are many different kinds of patterns in technical analysis: such as the cup and handle, ascending/descending channels, the head-and-shoulders pattern etc. Apart from the patterns, the technical analysts also use technical *indicators* and *oscillators.* An indicator is a mathematical calculation based on a securities price and/ or volumes, used to predict future prices. Common technical analysis indicators are the moving average convergence-divergence (MACD) indicator and the relative strength index (RSI). Oscillators are most advantageous when a clear trend cannot be easily seen in a company's stock such as when it trades horizontally or sideways. The most common oscillators are: the Stochastic oscillator, RSI (Relative Strength Index), PPO (Percentage Price Oscillator) and MFI (Money Flow Index).

The field of technical analysis is based on three assumptions:

1. The market discounts everything.
2 Price moves in trends.
3. History tends to repeat itself.

The price pattern, taking an example of Reliance Industries Ltd., from July 2008 at Rs.2400 has fallen to Rs.1117.25 in November 2008, is shown in Fig. 6

Technical Analysis assumes that the market is efficient and the price has already taken into consideration the other factors related to the company and the industry[7]. It is because of this assumption that many think technical analysis is a tool, which is effective for short-term investing. But the claims of the technical analysts are disputed by many academics, who claim

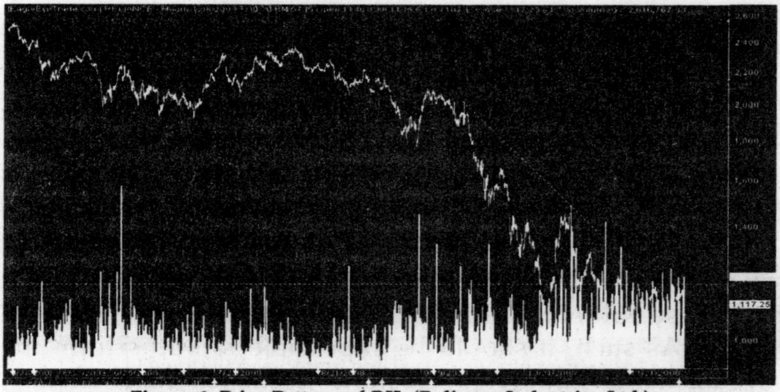

Figure 6: Price Pattern of RIL (Reliance Industries Ltd.)

that the evidence points rather to the random walk hypothesis, which states that the next change is not correlated to the last change.

Dow Theory

An attempt to trace the origins of technical analysis would inevitably lead to Dow theory. Dow theory remains the foundation of much of what we know today as technical analysis. Charles Dow, then editor of the Wall Street Journal, recognized that the movement is caused by the action/reaction of the people dealing in stocks rather than the news in itself.

The first basic premise of Dow theory suggests that all information - past, current and even future - is discounted into the markets and reflected in the prices of stocks and indexes[8]. That information includes everything from the emotions of investors to inflation and interest-rate data, along with pending earnings announcements to be made by companies after the close. From the prevailing trend in the market, the investor can make an investment decision. If the prevailing trend is upward, it follows that an investor would buy individual stocks trading at a fair valuation.

The three trends in Dow theory includes the primary or major trend lasting between one to three years; The secondary or intermediate trend is a correction of the primary trend lasting for a few weeks to months and finally the minor trend which are the corrective moves of the secondary trends which lasts from days to less than three weeks.

Efficient Market Hypothesis

Efficient markets are markets in which prices adjust quickly to new information and prices reflect the economic value of information. According to the Efficient Market Hypothesis (EMH), this means that stocks always trade at their fair value on stock exchanges, making it impossible for investors to either purchase undervalued stocks or sell stocks for inflated prices. As such, it should be impossible to outperform the overall market through expert stock selection or market timing, and that the only way an investor can possibly obtain higher returns is by purchasing riskier investments[9].

Although it is a cornerstone of modern financial theory, the EMH is highly controversial and often disputed. Believers argue it is pointless to search for undervalued stocks or to try to predict trends in the market through either fundamental or technical analysis. Meanwhile, while academics point to a large body of evidence in support of EMH, an equal amount of dissension also exists. For example, investors, such as Warren Buffett have consistently beaten the market over long periods of time, which by definition is impossible according to the EMH. Detractors of the EMH also point to events, such as the 1987 stock market crash when the Dow Jones Industrial Average (DJIA) fell by over 20% in a single day, as evidence that stock prices can seriously deviate from their fair values. The three degrees of EMH defends the theory as; (i) *Weak Form* of Efficiency claims all past prices of a stock are reflected in today's stock price. Therefore, technical analysis cannot be used to predict and beat a market. (ii) In the *strong form* of market efficiency, all information in a market, whether public or private, is accounted for in a stock price. Not even insider information could give an investor the advantage. (iii) the *semi-strong form* of efficiency, implies all public information is calculated into a stock's current share price which means that neither fundamental nor technical analysis can be used to achieve superior gains.

Random Walk Theory

The theory that stock price changes have the same distribution and are independent of each other, so the past movement or trend of a stock price or market cannot be used to predict its future movement[10]. In short, this is the idea that stocks take a random and unpredictable path. A follower of the random walk theory believes it's impossible to outperform the market without assuming additional risk. Critics of the theory, however, contend that stocks do maintain price trends over time-in other words, that it is possible to outperform the market by carefully selecting entry and exit points for equity investments[11].

The theory claims that day-to-day stock prices are independent of each other, meaning that momentum does not generally exist and calculations of past earnings growth does not predict future growth. The random walk theory also considers technical analysis undependable because, according to Malkiel, chartists buy only after price trends are established and sell only after price trends are broken; essentially, the chartists buy or sell too late and miss the boat. According to the theory, this happens because stock prices already reflect the information by the time the analyst moves on the stock[12]. Malkiel also notes that the widespread use of technical analysis reduces the advantages of the approach.

Further, Malkiel finds fundamental analysis flawed because analysts often collect bad or useless information and then poorly or incorrectly interpret that information when predicting stock values. Factors outside of a company or its industry may affect a stock price, rendering further the fundamental analysis irrelevant.

To conclude that the key element in creating market vibrations are investors behavior driven by their emotions, feelings and attitudes reflecting in the price movements of stock market and the indices. Against this backdrop this study proceeds to identify the behavioral factors and make an attempt to analyse the issues thereon in Chapters IV,V, VI and VII.

References

1. Sir John Templeton, "Golden Nuggets" (1997), Templeton Foundation Press, pp.22-23.
2. Susan Thomas, "India's Capital Markets: Have We Come Full Circle?", *Outlook* magazine, 14 January 2002.
3. Nupur Hetamsaria (2005), "What Indian Financial Markets Need", 12 April, 2005, www. Rediff.com/money.
4. B.Venkatachalam. Dr, Lecture Speech On "Currency Futures", conducted by MCX'SX and FKCCI on 12th January, 2009.
5. Eugene F, Fama (1965), "The Behavior of Stock Market Prices", *Journal of Business*, Vol. 38, No. 1., pp. 34 - 45.
6. William Goetzmann and Alok Kumar. "Diversification Decisions of Individual Investors and Asset Prices." 14 January 2004, pp. 1-58.
7. Maurice Kendall (1953), "The Analysis of Economic Time- Series- Part I: Prices", Journal of the Royal Statistical Society, Vol.116, No.1, pp. 11–34.
8. James Dow and Gary Gorton (1997), "Stock Market Efficiency and Economic Efficiency: Is There a Connection?", *The Journal of Finance*, Vol.LII, No.3, pp.1087 -1127.
9. Basu, S. (1977), "Investment Performance of Common Stocks in relation to their Price-Earnings Ratio: A Test of the Efficient Market Hypothesis", The Journal of Finance, Vol.32, No.3, pp. 663 - 674.
10. Malkiel, Burton G. (1973), "A Random Walk Down Wall Street" W.W. Norton & Company, Inc. pub., 6th edn., pp.45-48.
11. Maurice G. Kendall and B. Babington Smith (1938), "Randomness and Random Sampling Numbers," Journal of the Royal Statistical Society, Vol. 101:1, pp. 147-166.
12. Fama, Eugene F. (1965), "Random Walks In Stock Market Prices", *Financial Analysts Journal*, Vol.21, No. 5, pp. 55–59.
13. www. stockmarketguide.org
14. www. livemint.com
15. www.pib.nic.in
16. www.thehindubusinessline.com
17. www.icmrindia.org

18. www.envestindia.com
19. www.theskilledinvestor.com
20. www.capmarketline.com
21. www.investoguide.com
22. www. cime.com
23. www.stockteacher.com
24. www.jstor.org

3

Behavioral Finance – A Conceptual Analysis and Review of Research Studies

Several researchers have attempted to find whether heuristic[i] behaviour would help investors to beat the market. There has not been valid solutions substantiating, to make money from the rational shortcomings or heuristics[1]. Robert Schiller (2000), in his "Irrational Exuberance"[ii], has predicted the bubble crash[iii] but was not sure when it would burst. Even the technical or fundamental analysts are unable to deploy a strategy to beat the market. But it has been a proved fact that purely the human psychology causes market prices and fundamental values to diverge. Over a period of time the investors understand their mistakes and help them to take cautious moves so that the risk taken by them would, to some extent, minimize their losses.

Investors often experience various emotions such as optimism, pessimism, hope, fear, intuitive feeling, regret, over confidence etc. at varied degrees at different situations leading to a positive or a negative result. They become overly optimistic regarding their future prospects following a successful investment experience or conversely, if they have lost money, they become more myopic in their aversion to future potential losses. In this context examining how people's emotions affect their investment decisions and performance of successful investing leads to the study of Behavioral Finance. It has a critical implication in determining the investment success or failure than the investor's intellect. Warren Buffet (1999) agrees, "Success in investing doesn't correlate with IQ. Once you have ordinary intelligence, what you need is the temperament to control the urges that get other people into trouble in investing".

Numerous studies have shown that human beings are extraordinarily irrational about managing money specifically, investing in stock market. On any such investing decision-making, people attempt to simplify the complexity of the situation and arrive at a quick judgment using mental shortcuts. This irrationality in making decisions, especially in money matters, they tend to make several mistakes or errors. The mistakes or errors in judgment may take the following types:

- Herding behavior[iv]
- Excessive aversion to loss
- Fear of making incorrect decision
- Anchoring[v] on irrelevant data
- Reluctance to admit mistakes
- Overconfidence in beating the market
- Greed to multiply returns
- Tend to seek only information that confirms their opinions/decisions
- Believe that their investment success is due to their wisdom rather than the market trend
- Failing to assess their investment time horizon

For instance, the investors who feel confidence in their own skills and judgment in investing, may tend to prove others that they are capable of beating the market. Others who lack confidence would trade on noise (caused by actions of others) as if it were information. Statman (1987)[2] suggests that this attitude induces investors to trade more frequently, than on their own individual decisions. In light of the above discussion, attempt has been made in this chapter to highlight the evolution and significance of Behavioral Finance and portrays the major findings on the studies relevant to Behavioral Finance in the following pages.

Evolution of Behavioral Finance

Investors are expected to make decisions in every walk of life in choosing the best alternative especially in the field of finance. The decisions on financial investment and its background have been thoroughly analyzed by many economists, financial theoreticians and investment analysts. The analysts from capitalist countries have propounded the classical and modern theory. The classical theory, advocated by 'Adams Smith' (1776) through his 'Market Economy' concept has been further improved by Eugene Fama (1970), through his 'Efficient Market Hypothesis[3]', which was the first financial theory, which came into existence. This theory advocates that all investment decisions reflect all available information in the stock prices and the expected return[vi] is based on the market behavior. According to his argument the financial decisions are not based on the economic theory of demand and supply. His theory construed that investors were rational and their decision was based on the information available to them in the market and the price of the stocks was solely influenced by the market. EMH theory was replaced with a behavioral theory by the investigators in Behavioral finance in later years. Now the theory of Behavioral Finance has come into stay to predict the market behavior.

So, though EMH may be partially true to the extent that the market responds to new information, it is clear that information is not the only variable affecting the stock prices. Hence it is concluded that the security prices could deviate from their equilibrium values due to various psychological factors referred as 'Anomalies' which do not come under the paradigm and purview of EMH.

The central challenge to the EMH theory, is the existence of stock market anomalies affecting the stock prices, which play a key role in the volatility of market. Anomalies are considered to be reliable, widely known as inexplicable factors, implicit in returns, which refuted the theory of efficient markets. In this context, it is in need to discuss some of the pertinent anomalies tend to be existing in the market.

Anomalies in Stock Market Due to Some Behavioral Implications

Calendar Effect

Normally referred as 'January effect', indicate that higher returns can be earned in the first month compared to the rest of the year. Higher mean returns earned in January than in other months (Rozeff and Kinney, 1976)

Weekend Effect

Referred as 'Monday effect' or 'blue Monday' suggests that buying stocks on Friday afternoon or Monday morning is not advisable, since the investors tend to be selling at slightly higher prices. The returns were found to be negative on Mondays whereas positive on the other days of the week (French, 1980)

Size Effect

Also termed as 'Small-Firm effect'. Research Studies in this effect has revealed that small firms offer higher stock returns than large firms. The excess returns would have been earned by holding stocks of low capitalization companies (Banz,1981)

P/E Ratio Effect

The investor holding a low price to earnings ratio portfolio, has earned higher returns than stock of high P/E ratio

Noise-Trading

'Noise' (Fisher Black), causes markets to be inefficient, but often prevents us from taking advantage of inefficiencies. Investors who trade on the basis of imperfect information exhibit an irrational behavior, as against the rational speculators or arbitrageurs, who trade on the basis of information or noise-trading (Shleifer and Summers, 1990). Noise traders cause prices to deviate from their equilibrium values, where arbitrageurs tend to play the crucial role of stabilizing prices.

Over/Under Reaction

Stock prices over- or under-react to earnings announcement. The research conducted by DeBondt and Thaler (1985, 1987), revealed the stock prices over-reacting to the earnings developments. Bernard (1993), suggest that information is not impounded in prices instantaneously as EMH predicted, but only based on the higher or lesser of earnings of the companies.

Is Irrational Behaviour an Anomaly?

As mentioned earlier, behavioral finance theories directly conflict with traditional finance academicians. Both theories attempt to explain the behaviour and its implications of an investor.

The theory that most overtly opposes behavioral finance is the efficient market hypothesis, associated with Fama and Ken French. Their theory depends on the premise that investors are rational, whereas the theory of behavioral finance argues that the investor's behaviour are irrational due to 'emotional reasoning' and various 'anomalies' in the market.

EMH proponents argue that events those dealt with in behavioral finance are just short-term anomalies, and that over a long-term period those anomalies disappear with a return to market efficiency. Thus, there may not be enough evidence to suggest that market efficiency could be abandoned since empirical evidence has shown that markets tend to correct themselves over the long-term. This is evident from the reversal of a down-turn market, correcting within a short period of time.

Peter Bernstein[6] (1996), "While it is important to understand that the market doesn't work the way classical models think. There is a lot of evidence of herding, the behavioral finance concept of investors irrationally following the same course of action". In reality, markets are neither perfectly efficient nor completely inefficient. Peter Bernstein concludes, "the efficient market is a state of nature dreamed up by theoreticians. Neat, elegant, even majestic, it has nothing to do with the real world of uncertainty."

In furtherance of the research, Daniel Kahnemann and Amos Tversky (2001), found that both earlier theories, namely

EMH and CAPM is not applicable always and claimed that the investment decisions were purely on 'Psychological behavior' and 'Mental Accounting' of the investors. This concept then lead to the development of 'Behavioral Finance' in the investment field. The theory on Behavioral Finance has drawn the attention of researchers in recent years.

It appears that the knowledge level and processing of information varies from person to person. Inadequacy in the levels of knowledge and abilities to process information leads to situations termed as 'uncertain'/ 'random'/ 'probablistic'/ or 'chance', when the decisions taken may or may not be biased. This behavior in financial decisions is deduced as "imperfect rationality"[8] (Bernartzi –Thaler, 1999), which results in errors of judgment in decision-making.

The errors in judgment causes biases in decision-making may be described as "cognitive illusions". The cognitive illusion coupled with emotional reasoning of investors may sometime cause biases in judgment. Howard Raiffa (1988)[9], pointed out the three approaches to 'analysis of decisions'. The first approach termed as *'Normative Analysis'* is concerned with the rational solution to the decision problem in which actual decisions shall strive to approximate. *'Descriptive analysis'*, is the manner in which real people actually make decisions. Finally, the *'Prescriptive Analysis'*, is concerned with the practical advice that help people to make more rational decisions.

'Financial Advising', falls under the prescriptive activity, which helps to guide investors to make decisions that serve their interests, to eliminate biases of judgment. Investment decisions are based on instincts and not information.[10]. Financial decisions are made in situations of high complexity and high uncertainty, that compel the decision-maker to rely on intuition. Intuitions play a crucial role in most investment decisions. Kahnemann identifies a cluster of related biases and cognitive illusions in intuitive judgment termed as "Behavioral Heuristics"[11] (or mental shortcuts) that may result in wrong decisions. The above conceptual clarification on Behavioral Finance give room for the present study to highlight some of the interesting findings of the studies on the theory of Behavioral Finance.

Review of Research Studies

Julie R.Agnew (2006)[12], in his study, investigated whether some individuals are prone to behavioral biases in their 401(k) investments, using demographic data and allocation information for over 73000 employees, to examine two allocation biases and a participation bias. The findings suggested that higher salaried employees tend to make significantly better choices and participants who earn $100000 hold 12.7% less in company stock, are 3% less likely to follow the framing 1/n heuristic ,and are 37.7% more likely to participate than those earning $46000. Women make better choices in two of the three cases and he also found evidence of mental accounting.

Ou Hu, (2007)[13] has tested the common practice as the estimates of the next period factor premiums, generating inaccurate estimates and he had proposed an alternative way to estimate factor premium by using the structure variables that are important predictors of future assets returns.

Philip S. Russel and Violet M. Torbey (2002), in their article, "The Efficient Market Hypothesis on Trial: A Survey", in Business Quest, have attempted to put on trial, the Efficient Market Hypothesis, subjected to critical re-examination. The preliminary evidence indicates that the initial confidence in the EMH might have been misplaced. It is observed that financial equilibrium models based on EMH fail to depict trading operations in the real world. Various anomalies and inconsistent results call for refinement of the existing paradigm. It was proposed by the authors that a more coherent theory of stock market behavior can be developed by incorporating Keynesian ideologies on the speculative behavior of investors.

Daniel Kahneman and Mark W. Riepe (1998)[14], have tested the theory of 'Financial Advising' through the Prescriptive Analysis with an objective to guide investors to make decisions that best serve their interests, correlating , cognitive illusions and decision-making to avoid the biases of judgment in their investments. The effectiveness in dealing with the judgment biases, was discussed with a cluster of related biases and cognitive illusions in intuitive judgment that are most likely to affect investment decisions. Investors who are prone to these biases will take risks that he does not acknowledge , experience outcomes that they did not anticipate, will be prone to unjustified trading, and may end up blaming themselves or others when outcomes are bad. Various elements of investor behavior like Over-Confidence, Optimism, Over-reaction, hindsight, Narrow Framing, Regrets of Omission and Commission and Risk-Taking were analyzed exposed to several alternatives of investments and decision-making.

Charles M.C.Lee, Andrei Shleifer, and Richard H.Thaler (1991)[15], examined the proposition that fluctuations in discounts of closed end funds are driven by changes in individual investor sentiment. The theory implies that discounts on various funds move together, that new funds get started when seasoned funds sell at a premium or a small discount, and that discounts are correlated with prices of other securities affected by the same investor sentiment. They concluded that both closed-end funds and small stocks tend to be held by individual investors, and that the discounts on closed-end funds narrow when small stocks do well.

Russel J.Fuller (1996)[16], comprehended the research of Amos Tversky and Kahneman on their work on ' Prospect Theory'. This theory based on the simple notion that the pain associated with a given amount of loss is greater than the pleasure derived by an equivalent gain. They also discussed about the anomalous behavior of investors avoiding the realization of losses and selling winners too early.

Paul Willman (2000)[17], reviewed Peter Bernstein's work on the risk patterns and the relationship of risk and return in his book, "Against the Gods: The remarkable story of Risk" has also highlighted that the heuristics and cognitive biases of investors discussed in Hersh Shefrin's book, on " Beyond Greed and Fear: Understanding Behavioral Finance and Psychology of Investing". The author highlights the three themes discussed in this book, (1) that relates to the biased beliefs that predispose them to commit errors; (2) narrow-framing on gains or losses; and (3) how the above two items cause market prices to deviate from fundamental values. He also discusses on the impact of price earnings and the speculative bubble in 1989 from Robert J. Shiller's, book on "Irrational Exuberance".

Andrea Devenow, Ivowelch (1996)[18], briefly describes the economics of rational herding in financial markets. Some models can predict perfect herding, in which rational agents all act alike without any countervailing force. Such herding typically arises either from direct payoff externalities, principal-agent problems or informational learning. The author provides a few pointers to related literature and suggests issues to be addressed in future research.

AnoopKumar (2005)[19], classified cognitive biases or adoption of mental models, used in heuristic decision processes. The biases resulting from the use of heuristics include; Availability Bias , Overconfidence, Anchoring, Gambler's fallacy. Some of the mental frames that caused investors to make errors of judgment include: Loss of Regret Aversion and Mental Accounting. The author classified the investors as 'Value-Managers' who exploit investor's over-reaction and 'Momentum managers' who exploit investor's under-reaction.

Peter W. Hom, Angelo S. DeNisi, Angelo J.Kinicki and Brender D. Bannister (1982)[20], compared a Behaviorally Anchored Rating Scale (BARS) optimal procedure developed by Bernardin, Lashells and Smith & Alvares (1976) with a carefully constructed summated rating scale. Using both scale formats (designed to evaluate teaching effectiveness), 859 undergraduates rated 32 instructors during spring classes and 314 undergraduates rated 19 instructors during summer classes. Analysis of covariance revealed no format effect on the performance ratings obtained during the second rating period in the spring experiment. BARS feedback however, produced greater behavioral change among ratees than did feedback from the alternative format used during the summer experiment.

Michael Theobald, (1995)[21], have attempted to review briefly the current position of 'Capital Asset Pricing Theory' and testing to consider the implications for portfolio managers.

The author concludes that CAPM provides positive implications regarding the structure of equilibrium returns for risky assets; these implications are relatively robust to the underlying assumptions necessary to drive the CAPM.

Richard Dobbins and Stephen F. Witt (1995)[22] , asserts that share prices fully reflect all available information, any new or shock information being very rapidly incorporated into the share price. This hypothesis has very powerful implications for investment analysis and corporate management.

Macro Cipriani and Antonio Guarino (2002)[23], studied whether herding can arise in a laboratory financial market in which agents trade sequentially. Agents trade an asset whose value is unknown and whose price is efficiently set by a market maker. They attempted to show that the presence of a price mechanism destroys the possibility of herding. Most agents followed their private information and prices converge to the fundamental value. This result contrasted with the case of a fixed price, where herding and cascades arise. When the price moves, however, agents may behave as contrarian ie., they may trade against the market, something not accounted for by the theory. Finally, they studied whether informational cascades arise when trade is costly (eg. Because of a tobin tax). With trade costs, most subjects rationally decided not to trade and the price was unable to aggregate private information efficiently.

William Brock, Josef lakonishok and Blake Lebaron (1992)[24], tested two of the simplest and most popular trading rules-moving average and trading range break by utilizing the Dow Jones Index from 1897 to 1986. Overall, their results provided strong support for the technical strategies. The returns obtained from these strategies are not consistent with four popular null models: the random walk, the Garch -M and the Exponential GARCH. Buy signals consistently generate higher returns than sell signals, and further , the returns following buy signals are less volatile than returns following sell signals. Moreover returns following sell signals are negative, which is not easily explained by any of the currently existing equilibrium models.

Stephen P ferris, Robert A Haugen and Anil K Makhija (1988)[25], have provided an empirical evidence comparing two models of trading in equities–the well known tax-loss selling hypothesis and the 'disposition effect'. According to the disposition effect, investors are reluctant to realize losses but are eager to realize gains. Their study distinguishes between the two models with a new methodology that examines the relationship between volume at a given point in time and volume that took place in the past at different stock prices. The evidence overwhelmingly supports the disposition effect not only as a determinant of year-end volume, but also as a determinant of volume levels throughout the year.

Michael Kaestner (2006)[26], have explained two kinds of anomalies in Behavioral Finance as a determinant of asset pricing. Ie., under-reaction and over-reaction established by an impressive record of empirical work. While under-reaction defines a slow adjustment of prices to corporate events or announcements, over-reaction deals with extreme stock price reactions to previous information or past performance. The author has investigated the current and past earnings surprises and subsequent market reactions for listed US companies over the period 1983-1999. The results suggested that investors simultaneously exhibit short-term under reaction to 'earnings announcements' and long-term over-reaction to 'past highly unexpected earnings'.

R. D'Hulst and G.J.Rodgers (1999)[27], studied on herding instinct by developing an exact solution presented to a model that mimics the crowding effect in financial markets which arises when groups of agents share information. The authors showed that the size distribution of groups of agents has a power low tail with an exponential cut-off. As the size of these groups determine the supply and demand balance, this implies heavy tails in the distribution of price variation. The moments of the distribution are calculated as well as the kurtosis. They found that the kurtosis is large for all model parameter values and that the model is not self-organizing.

In his study, on " The Anomaly of size: Does it really matter?", *Ian M Dobbs*[28], suggested that size-related regularities in asset prices (size, leverage, book to market equity etc.) should not be regarded as anomalies. He has clarified that the argument for size-related variables is necessarily mis-specified, followed by assessing the likely quantitative magnitude of this type of bias in a simulation study calibrated on US data.

Chiaku Chukwuogor-Ndu[29] has examined the financial markets' trends such as the annual returns, daily returns and volatility of returns in 15 emerging and developed European financial markets. A set of parametric and non-parametric tests is used to test the equality of mean returns and standard deviations of the returns. Although positive annual index closing price changes were the norm between 1997 and 2004, many of the European indexes experienced negative changes especially in 1998 and 2002. It is important to note that between 1999 and 2000, the Russian MTM and the Turkish XU, 100 achieved astronomical growth. There was presence of the day of the week effect during the period 1007-2004. Seven of the European Financial markets experienced negative returns on Monday and seven others also experience negative returns on Wednesday. There was generally high volatility of returns in the European markets. The results of the *Levene's* (1960) test of the equality of standard deviations of the returns at the 5 percent confidence level could not reject the Null Hypothesis that mean returns are equal across the days of the week for all the markets except for MBTEL, Italy.

Kenneth Ryack; Thomas Kida,[30] have argued that, given the Volume of Data Analyzed in Investment Decisions, Analysts and Investors often must Rely on their Memory of Financial Information. Prior Research Suggests that Differences in the Amount of Information Used by Investors may Affect their Valuation of Securities and Market Prices. Thus, Factors Influencing the Amount and Accuracy of Information Recalled could Impact Estimates of Stock Value and Market Prices. Financial Information is often Presented in Different Formats. This Study Examines Whether Differences in Format Presentation at Encoding and Retrieval Affect the Recall of Financial Data. They also Investigated, whether memory for

Financial Information can be Improved with a Simple Technique that Uses Mental Imagery to Reinstate the Original Encoding Conditions. They had found that even a Minor Change in the Presentation Format has Significant Effects on memory for Financial Information. Their Results suggested that the Use of Mental Imagery to Reinstate the Original Format may significantly improve memory for Financial Data.

In the Aftermath of the Enron Corporation Failure, *Harry F. Griffin* [31], acknowledged that many Investors Experienced a Financial Loss when their Enron Equity Holdings Lost Market Value. Their Research Centers upon the Loss of that Market Value, and when the Capital Market first Signaled the Positive Potential of that Loss. An Examination of Enron Option Open Interest from January 1, 2000 through December 31, 2001 Reveals that such Information was Available, Observable, and Inferential a Year Earlier.

The results of an asset market experiment, in which sixty-four subjects trade two assets on eight markets in a computerized continuous double auction, indicate that objectively irrelevant information influences trading behavior. *Erich Kirchler; Boris Maciejovsky; Martin Weber*[32], found that positively and negatively framed information leads to a particular trading pattern, but leaves trading prices and volume unaffected. The experiment also provided support for the disposition effect. Participants who experience a gain sell their assets more rapidly than participants who experience a loss, and positively framed subjects generally sell their assets later than negatively framed subjects.

As is well-known, investors are subject to overconfidence. Using a survey of about 2,000 defined contribution pension plan members, *Gokul Bhandari; Richard Deaves*[33] not only corroborate this, but also explore the demographics of this behavioral flaw. Noting that overconfidence can be partitioned into certainty and knowledge, they have found that highly-educated males who are nearing retirement, who have received investment advice, and who have experience investing for themselves, tend to have a higher certainty level. For some groups knowledge matches certainty. They concluded that the highly-educated males are more subject to overconfidence.

Douglas Jordan; J. David Diltz [34], studied the disposition effect referred as the tendency to hold losing investments and sell profitable ones. They examined day trader transactions for evidence of a disposition effect and found that approximately 65% of sample traders hold losing trades longer than profitable ones, providing evidence that sample day traders display the disposition effect.

Franco Caparrelli; Anna Maria D'Arcangelis; Alexander Cassuto[35] The authors studied the herding effect in the capital markets. Using data from the Italian Stock Exchange, the authors test for the presence of herding as described in Christie and Huang [1995], Chang, Cheng, and Khorana [2000], and Hwang and Salmon [2001]. The tests support Christie and Huang's conclusions that herding is present in extreme market conditions.

Rank Westerhoff [36], has developed a simple behavioral exchange rate model in which investor perception of the fundamental value is anchored to the nearest round number. Traders adjust their anchors in two ways. Some believe that exchange rates move toward (perceived) fundamentals, while others bet on a continuation of the current exchange rate trend. The behavior of the traders causes complex dynamics. Since the exchange rate tends to circle around its perceived fundamental value, the foreign exchange market is persistently misaligned. Central authorities have the opportunity to reduce such distortions by pushing the exchange rate to less biased anchors, but to achieve this, they have to break psychological barriers between anchors.

The attraction effect occurs when an inferior item changes a decision-maker's perception of the relationship between other available alternatives, contrary to the expectations of rational decision-making. *David L. Schwarzkopf* [37], presents the first evidence that this effect, which has appeared persistently in consumer research, could influence investment decisions. They also found, two distinct patterns of reaction to the inferior item as a sign of "cluster attraction"-a way of spreading investment risk. Evidence of attraction means that the values of important facets of corporate reporting may not be stable across an investor's decisions, but may depend on the items presently available for investment. Results of an experiment conducted with approximately 100 graduate students with investing experience or interest show that the investor's perceived values of reported financial or non-financial performance, quality of earnings, and information source reliability are subject to trade-offs and can be altered by the composition of the decision set, rather than by any intrinsic change in the investment candidate itself. The discussion highlighted the implications of these findings for an understanding of how investors regard the qualities of financial reporting.

Several studies have assessed stock market under- or overreaction of stocks and there is some agreement among them. However, there is much disagreement about what constitutes market under reaction or overreaction, and the conditions that cause it. The substantial variation in results among studies may be partially attributed to the types of firms that are contained in any sample. *Aigbe Akhigbe; Stephen J. Larson; Jeff Madura*[38], investigated this premise by focusing on a sample of technology stocks that experienced an extreme change in stock price, along with a corresponding control sample of non-technology stocks that experienced a similar extreme change in stock price on the same day. Based on the subsequent stock price behavior of each sample, a greater degree of overreaction within extreme positive changes in technology stock prices (winners) than in non-technology stock prices was identified. When considering winners and losers collectively for technology and non-technology firms, it appeared that the market was overoptimistic when it initially revalues technology stock prices relative to non-technology stock prices. The degree of under-or overreaction of technology stocks varied within the sample of technology stocks, and conditioned on firm-specific characteristics. Overall, the authors suggest that technology stocks exhibit unique stock price behavior subsequent to an extreme change in price, and that this unique behavior can even vary among technology firms according to firm-specific characteristics.

Richard L. Peterson[39], attempted to examine the relationship between investor psychology and security pricing around anticipated events. Taking a multidisciplinary approach, the authors pull together research in the finance, psychology, and neuroscience literature. Event studies in the finance literature demonstrate anomalous security (stock, commodity, bond, or option) price movements around the dates of anticipated events. According to the authors, the neuroscience literature demonstrates correlations between reward anticipation and the arousal of affect (feelings, emotions, moods, attitudes, and preferences). In the cognitive psychology literature there was evidence for the central role of affect in motivating investing behavior. They have outlined an investment strategy for exploiting the event-related security price pattern described by the trading strategy "buy on the rumor and sell on the news."

Tarek El-Sehity; Hans Haumer; Christian Helmenstein; Erich Kirchler; Boris Maciejovsky[40], have investigated the robustness of hindsight bias in experimental asset markets, the time-invariance of the different experimental risk elicitation methods of certainty equivalents and binary lottery choices, and their correspondence. Their results within-subject approach with 133 traders did not support the conjecture that hindsight bias is a general phenomenon. Furthermore, their findings challenge the presumption of time-stable risk preferences and of procedural invariance with respect to different experimental risk elicitation methods.

Philip Y.K. Cheng[41], in his article has Extended Previous Research on how Overconfidence Affects Trading Performance in Two Ways. First, he Examined whether the Degree of Impact is Different between an Electronic Trading Market (as in a Stock Market) and an Open Outcry Environment (as in a Futures Market). Second, he Examined the Impact of Overconfidence from the Perspective of Miscalibration, Market Confidence, the better than Average Effect, and Risk Attitudes. The Significant Findings (5%) Indicate that Higher Overconfidence Leads to Poorer Trading Performance Generally. However, the Degree of Impact is Higher in an Open Outcry Environment, where there are Visual, Verbal, and Emotional Interactions between Traders, than in an Electronic Trading Environment, where a Trader Operates Primarily in an Isolated Setting. Likewise, the Traders who Choose to Trade in an Open Outcry Environment are Generally more Overconfident than those who Trade in a more Isolated Setting.

Malcolm Baker; Jeffrey Wurgler[42], in an attempt to study how Investor Sentiment Affects the Cross-section of Stock Returns Predicted that a Wave of Investor Sentiment has Larger Effects on Securities whose Valuations are Highly Subjective and Difficult to Arbitrage. When Sentiment was high, on the other Hand, these Categories of Stock Earned a Relatively Low Subsequent Returns.

An attempt to find out, whether the "disposition Effect," that is the Tendency of Investors to Ride Losses and Realize Gains, Induces "underreaction" to News, Leading to Return Predictability, *Andrea Frazzini*[43], used data on Mutual Fund Holdings to Construct a New Measure of Reference Purchasing Prices for Individual Stocks, and it showed that Post-announcement Price Drift is most Severe whenever Capital Gains and the News Event have the same Sign. The Magnitude of the Drift Depends on the Capital Gains (losses) Experienced by the Stock Holders on the Event Date.

Alexander Ljungqvist; William J Wilhelm[44], attempted to derive a behavioral measure of the IPO decision-maker's satisfaction with the underwriter's performance based on Loughran and Ritter (2002) and assess its ability to explain the decision-maker's choice among underwriters in *subsequent* securities offerings. Controlling for other known factors, IPO firms are less likely to switch underwriters when our behavioral measure indicates they were satisfied with the IPO underwriter's performance. Underwriters also extract higher fees for subsequent transactions involving satisfied decision-makers.

Kent D. Miller And Zur Shapira[45], has drawn insights from behavioral decision theory to explain how managers value call and put options. Behavioral decision theory points to important deviations from the assumptions of normative option pricing models in finance. They collected option pricing data to test the behavioral hypotheses. The authors discussed on the implications of the findings for the management of real options and suggest directions for developing descriptive real option theory. Furthermore, these symbolic numbers are often referred to as *psychological barriers*. These effects are identified as a widespread phenomenon permeating into the economic decision making and financial market environments. *Jason Mitchell*[46], outlines various arguments and rationale from the cultural, economic, and behavioral literature why clustering and other effects such as psychological barriers may be expected in financial markets. Evidence across a variety of literatures suggests that financial market clustering derives from a variety of sources. There is evidence from a cultural and conventional basis to suggest that number preference exists and that there is a natural tendency to round that derives from the development of the modern decimal system. The literature also provides valid behavioral and economic reasons as to why these effects may occur.

John R. Nofsinger And Richard W. Sias[47], have documented strong positive correlation between changes in institutional ownership and returns measured over the same period. The result suggested that either institutional investors positive-feedback trade more than individual investors or institutional herding impacts prices more than herding by individual investors. They found that both factors play a role in explaining the relation. Moreover, institutional herding is positively correlated with lag returns and appears to be related to stock return momentum.

Kent Daniel, David Hirshleifer, And Avanidhar Subrahmanyam[48], have proposed a theory of securities market under- and overreactions based on two well-known psychological biases: investor overconfidence about the precision of private information; and biased self-attribution, which causes asymmetric shifts in investors' confidence as a function of their investment outcomes. According to them, overconfidence implies negative long-lag autocorrelations, excess volatility, and, when managerial actions are correlated with stock mispricing, public-event-based return predictability. Biased self-attribution adds positive short-lag autocorrelations, short-run earnings "drift," but negative correlation between future returns and long-term past stock market and accounting performance.

Imad A. Moosa[49], have investigated the seasonality in U.S. stock prices using monthly average data on the Dow Jones Industrial Average over the period 1970-2005. Their results revealed the presence of a significant January effect except in the most recent period, 1990-2005, when a strong negative July effect surfaced. This finding was confirmed by using a more sophisticated structural time series model with an autoregressive structure. Some explanations are suggested for the disappearance of the January effect and the surfacing of the July effect.

Michael B. Clement And Senyo Y. Tse.[50], have classified in their study, that analysts' earnings forecasts as *herding* or *bold* and found that (1) boldness likelihood increases with the analyst's prior accuracy, brokerage size, and experience and declines with the number of industries the analyst follows, consistent with theory linking boldness with career concerns and ability; (2) bold forecasts are more accurate than herding forecasts; and (3) herding forecast revisions are more strongly associated with analysts' earnings forecast errors (actual earnings—forecast) than are bold forecast revisions.

Using a sample of New Zealand investors, *Alireza Tourani-Rad, Stephen Kirkby*[51], have investigated three behavioural finance theories: investor overconfidence, socialization and the familiarity effect. They found support for the investor overconfidence theory, using characteristics such as past success, optimism, confidence in one's abilities, investment experience and investment-related knowledge. Concerning the socialization theory, they observed that the investors actively sought information regarding the stock market, 75 per cent doing this on a weekly basis. Those investors that kept themselves informed daily outperformed other investors by 8 per cent. *Allen M. Poteshman*[52], investigated options market reaction to changes in the instantaneous variance of the underlying asset. The main findings of his study was, First, options market investors underreact to individual daily changes in instantaneous variance. Second, these same investors overreact to periods of mostly increasing or mostly decreasing daily changes in instantaneous variance. Third, they tend to underreact ~overreact! to current daily changes in instantaneous variance that are preceded mostly by daily changes of the opposite ~same! sign. The third finding reconciled the first two and consistent with well-established cognitive biases.

Balasingham Balachandran, Tuan Anh Nguyen[53], have examined the impact of the announcement of special dividends for a sample of Australian companies over the period July 1989 to June 2002. The risk-adjusted price reaction to special dividend announcements from the day before the announcement to the day after the announcement (day 1 to day 1) is positive and statistically significant, averaging 3.67 per cent. Initial special dividend announcements (4.68 per cent) led to stronger price reaction than special dividend announcements that follow an earlier special dividend (1.51 per cent) in the previous year. The magnitude of price reactions to special dividend announcements is statistically related to the size of the special dividend, the existence of prior special dividend announcements, abnormal cash flow for the year ended after the special dividend announcement, the existence of dividend reinvestment plans (DRP) versus non-DRP, and a preannouncement effect.

According to *George M. Constantinides*[54], the mean, covariability, and predictability of the return of different classes of financial assets challenge the rational economic model for an explanation. The unconditional mean aggregate equity premium is almost seven percent per year and remains high after adjusting downwards the sample mean premium by introducing prior beliefs about the stationarity of the price-dividend ratio and the non- forecastability of the long-term dividend growth and price-dividend ratio. Using a unique database of daily trading activity, *David R. Gallagher, Adrian Looi*[55], have examined the ability of active Australian equity managers to earn superior risk-adjusted returns. They found evidence of superior trade performance, where performance is a function of stock size. The findings indicated that active equity managers are able to successfully exploit private information more readily in stocks ranked 101–150 by market-cap, where the degree of analyst coverage, information flows and market efficiency are lower than for large-cap stocks.

Werner Antweiler And Murray Z. Frank[56], studied the effect of more than 1.5 million messages posted on Yahoo! Finance and Raging Bull about the 45 companies in the Dow Jones Industrial Average and the Dow Jones Internet Index. Bullishness is measured using computational linguistics methods. *Wall Street Journal* news stories are used as controls. They found that stock messages helped predict market volatility. Their effect on stock returns is statistically significant but economically small. Consistent with Harris and Raviv (1993), disagreement among the posted messages is associated with increased trading volume.

Mahdi M. Hadi[57], reported that the objective of accounting numbers is to provide the financial data about the performance of certain enterprise in order to help the managers, investors, shareholders and government authorities in making their decisions. On the other hand, the purpose of accounting research is to evaluate the usefulness of accounting data to investors and other users. Furthermore, the purpose of capital market research is to examine the association between accounting numbers and security return and to test whether or not accounting data carry any information content to security market, and if so it should be impounded in the security price, the results had shown the security market reacted with mixed signal on releasing profitability, liquidly, and solvency information.

Edwin J. Elton, Martin J. Gruber, And Jeffrey A. Busse[58], have shown that selecting funds based on low expenses or high past returns outperforms the portfolio of index funds selected by investors. Their results exemplify the fact that, in a market where arbitrage is not possible, dominated products can prosper.

In their study, *David Hirshleifer*[59], have suggested that the basic paradigm of asset pricing is in vibrant flux. The purely rational approach is being subsumed by a broader approach based upon the psychology of investors. In this approach, security expected returns are determined by both *risk* and *misevaluation*. This survey sketches a framework for understanding decision biases, evaluates the a priori arguments and the capital market evidence bearing on the importance of investor psychology for security prices, and reviews recent models.

Joshua D. Coval And Tyler Shumway[60], have analyzed the information content of the ambient noise level in the Chicago Board of Trade's 30-year Treasury Bond futures trading pit. Controlling for a variety of other variables, including lagged price changes, trading volumes, and news announcements, they found that the sound level conveys information which is highly economically and statistically significant. Specifically, changes in the sound level forecast changes in the cost of transacting. Following a rise in the sound level, prices become more volatile, depth declines, and information asymmetry increases.

In their paper, *Allenm. Poteshmanandvitaly Serbin*[61], have analyzed the early exercise of exchange-traded options by different classes of investors over the 1996 to 1999 period. A large number of exercises are identified as clearly irrational without invoking any model of market equilibrium. Customers of discount brokers and customers of full-service brokers both engage in a significant number of irrational exercises while traders at large investment houses exhibit no irrational early exercise behavior.

To contribute to the literature on the valuation of initial public offerings (IPOs). In particular, to test the presence of over-optimism when pricing IPOs on the Italian Nuovo Mercato, *Stefano Paleari and Silvio Vismara*[62], investigated whether the analysts make systematic errors when forecasting the performance of the firm undergoing the IPO by comparing analysts' exante expectations to actual ex-post figures. Using a sample of pre-IPO analysts' reports, with regression analysis using the forecast errors (FE) of post-issue sales as dependent variable in order to find out the determinants of mis-valuation.

Nicholas Barberis And Ming Huang[63], have studied equilibrium firm-level stock returns in two economies: one in which investors are loss averse over the fluctuations of their stock portfolio, and another in which they are loss averse over the fluctuations of individual stocks that they own. Both approaches had shed light on empirical phenomena, and found the second approach to be more successful: In that economy, the typical individual stock return had a high mean and excess volatility, with a large value premium in the cross section captured by a commonly used multifactor model.

Joshua D. Coval And Tyler Shumway[64], documented a strong evidence for behavioral biases among Chicago Board of Trade proprietary traders and investigated the effect these biases had on prices. The traders appeared highly loss-averse, regularly assuming above-average afternoon risk to recover from morning losses. However, the market appeared to distinguish these risk-seeking trades from informed trading. Prices set by loss-averse traders are reversed significantly more quickly than those set by unbiased traders.

Harrison Hong And Jeremy C. Stein[65], had propounded a model of a market populated by two groups of boundedly rational agents: "news watchers" and "momentum traders." Each news watcher observes some private information, but fails to extract other news watchers' information from prices. If information diffuses gradually across the population, prices under react in the short run. The under reaction means that the momentum traders can profit by trend chasing.

Applying a unique data set to monitor the buys, sells, and holds of individuals and institutions in the Finnish stock market on a daily basis, *Mark grinblatt and matti keloharju*[66], employed Logit regressions to identify the determinants of buying and selling activity over a two-year period and evidenced that investors are reluctant to realize losses, that they engage in tax-loss selling activity, and that past returns and historical price patterns, such as being at a monthly high or low, affect trading and found that life-cycle trading plays a role in the pattern of buys and sells.

If arbitrage is costly and noise traders are active, asset prices may deviate from fundamental values for long periods of time. *Gordon Gemmill And Dylan C. Thomas*[67], used a sample of 158 closed-end funds to show that noise-trader sentiment, as proxied by retail-investor flows, lead to fluctuations in the discount. They found that funds which are more difficult to arbitrage had larger discounts, due to the censoring of the discount by the arbitrage bounds, and the freedom of managers to increase charges when arbitrage is costly.

Michael F. Fergusonand Richard L. Shockleyn[68], reported that many empirical "anomalies" are actually consistent with the single beta capital asset pricing model if the empiricist utilizes an equity-only proxy for the true market portfolio. Equity betas estimated against this particular inefficient proxy will be understated, with the error increasing with the leverage. Thus, specific variables that correlate with leverage (such as book-to-market and size) appeared to explain returns after controlling for proxy beta simply because they captured the missing beta risk

Unlike the 1987 stock market crash, the 1997 stock market decline was clearly preceded by new information that affected fundamental values of U.S. firms. *David Michayluk, Karyn L. Neuhauser*[69], provided a detailed description of U.S. stock returns surrounding the Asian financial crisis. Consistent with the overreaction hypothesis, they found strong evidence of a magnitude effect in short-term return reversals. Additionally, they evidenced short-term return predictability in the aftermath. The results were robust to controls for size, price, risk, and bid-ask bounce effects. Overall, the results were indicative of investor overreaction in times of market crisis.

Milton Friedman argued that irrational traders will consistently lose money, will not survive, and, therefore, cannot influence long-run asset prices. Since his work, survival and price impact have been assumed to be the same. In this paper, *Leonid Kogan, Stephen A. Ross, Jiang Wang, And Mark M. Westerfield*[70], demonstrated that survival and price impact are two independent concepts. The price impact of irrational traders does not rely on their long-run survival, and they can have a significant impact on asset prices even when their wealth becomes negligible. They also showed that irrational traders' portfolio policies can deviate from their limits long after the price process approaches its long-run limit.

Chiaku Chukwuogor-Ndu[71], examined the financial markets' trends such as the annual returns, daily returns and volatility of returns in 15 emerging and developed European financial markets. A set of parametric and non-parametric tests were used to test the equality of mean returns and standard deviations of the returns. Seven of the European Financial markets experienced negative returns on Monday and seven others also experienced negative returns on Wednesday. There was generally high volatility of returns in the European markets.

Alexander Ljungqvist And William J. Wilhelm, Jr.[72] derived a behavioral measure of the IPO decision-maker's satisfaction with the underwriter's performance based on Loughran and Ritter (2002) and assessed its ability to explain the decision-maker's choice among underwriters in *subsequent* securities offerings. Controlling for other known factors, IPO firms were less likely to switch underwriters when their behavioral measure indicated they were satisfied with the IPO underwriter's performance. Underwriters extract higher fees for subsequent transactions involving satisfied decision-makers.

Statman, Meir[73] argued that prior studies of diversification have underestimated the number of stocks needed to diversify portfolio, and discussed the theoretical implications of holding a randomly selected portfolio of 10 stocks, as opposed to 500. Cites data from Elton and Tamarkin [1977] indicating that the marginal cost of diversification does not exceed marginal utility until 100-200 stocks are held in the portfolio. The author finds that, after transaction costs are considered, the Vanguard Index Trust dominates a 35-stock portfolio for a borrowing investor and a 50-stock portfolio for a lending investor. The author notes that "the typical investor's stock portfolio contains only a small fraction of the available securities."

Conclusion

The above discussion on the concept of Behavioral Finance open the gateways for understanding the rational vis-à-vis irrational behavior of investors. Though several studies have revealed interesting relationship between the stock market and the different behaviors exhibited by the investors, there appears to be a vacuum existing in understanding the irrational behavior of investors in financial decision-making.

References

1. Robert J Shiller (2000), *"Irrational Exuberance"*, Princeton University Press.
2. Statman, Meir. (22, September 1987), "How Many Stocks Make a Diversified Portfolio?" *Journal of Financial and Quantitative Analysis.*
3. Eugene Fama (1970), "Efficient Capital Markets: A Review of Theory and Empirical Work", Journal of Finance, Vol.25, No.2, 383-417 and 1991, Efficient Capital Markets II, The Journal of Finance, Vol. 46, No.5, 1575-1617.
4. Louis Bachelier (1900), "The Theory of Speculation", Mathematical Finance, Blackwell Publishers, Vol 10, No. 3, 341-353.
5. Eugene Fama (1965), " The Behavior of Stock Market Prices", Journal of Business , 34-105. " Random Walks in Stock market prices", Financial Analysts Journal and in (1968), Institutional Investor.
6. Bernstein, Peter L. (1996), *Against The Gods: The Remarkable Story of Risk.* New York: John Wiley & Sons.
7. Sharpe, William F. (1964). "Capital Asset Prices - A Theory of Market Equilibrium Under Conditions of Risk". *Journal of Finance* **XIX** (3): 425–42.
8. Bernartzi, Shlomo and Richard H. Thaler (1999), "Risk Aversion or Myopia? Choices in Repeated Gambles and Retirement Investment." *Management Science* 45, 364-381.
9. David E. Bell, Howard Raiffa, Amos Tversky (1988), "Decision Making: Descriptive, Normative, and Prescriptive Interactions", Cambridge University Press.

10. Kahneman, D., & Riepe, M. (1998), "Aspects of Investor Psychology: Beliefs, Preferences and Biases Investment Advisors Should Know About", *The Journal of Portfolio Management, 24,* 52-65.

11. Kahneman, D., & Tversky, A. (1996), "On the Reality of Cognitive Illusions: A Reply to Gigerenzer's Critique", *Psychological Review, 103,* 582-591.

12. Julie R. Agnew, " Do Behavioral Biases Vary Across Individuals? Evidence from Individual Level 401(k) Data", *Journal of Financial and Quantitative Analysis,* Vol. 41, No. 4, December 2006, 939-962

13. Ou Hu (1991), "Applicability of the Fama - French Three Factor Model in Forecasting Portfolio Returns", *The Journal of Financial Research,* Vol.30, No.1, 111-127.

14. Daniel Kahneman; Mark W. Riepe (summer 1998) "Assets of Investor Psychology", *Journal of Portfolio Management,* Vol.24, No.4.

15. Charles M.C.Lee, Andrei Shleifer, and Richard H.Thaler (1991), "Investor Sentiment and the Closed-End Fund puzzle", *The Journal of Finance,* Vol. XLVI, No.1, 1991, 75-109.

16. Russel J.Fuller (1996), "Amos Tversky, Behavioral Finance and Nobel Prizes", *Financial Analyst Journal,* July/August, 7-8.

17. Paul Willman (2000), "Risk, Greed, Sound and Fury", *Business Strategy Review,* Vol.II, Issue 2, 72-74.

18. Andrea Devenow, Ivowelch (1996), "Rational Herding in Financial Economics", European Economic Review 40 (1996), 603-615.

19. AnoopKumar (2005), "Exploiting Behavioral Biases to Add Value", SEI Investment Developments Inc, Weekly Commentary, 2005.

20. Peter W. Hom, Angelo S. DeNisi, Angelo J.Kinicki and Brender D.Bannister (1982), "Effectiveness of Performance Feedback from Behaviorally Anchored Rating Scales", Journal of Applied Psychology, (1982), Vol. 67, No.5, 568- 576.

21. Michael Theobald (1995), "Capital Asset Pricing:Theory, Empirics, and Implications for Portfolio Management", Managerial Finance, Vol.5, No.1, pp 57 - 63.

22. Richard Dobbins and Stephen F.Witt (1995), "Some Implications of the EMH", Managerial Finance Vol.5, No.1, 65-79

23. Macro Cipriani and Antonio Guarino, (2002), "Herding and Price convergence in a laboratory Financial Market", 1-41.
24. William Brock, Josef Iakonishok and Blake Lebaron (1992), "Simple Technical Trading Rules and the Stochastic Properties of Stock Returns", Journal of Finance, Vol.5, 1731-1764.
25. Stephen P. Ferris, Robert A. Haugen and Anil k. Makhija (1988), "Predicting Contemprory Volume with Historic Volume at Differential Price Levels: Evidence supporting the Disposition Effect", Journal of Finance, Vol XLIII, No.3, 677-698.
26. Michael Kaestner (2006), "Investors' Misreaction to Unexpected Earnings: Evidence of Simultaneous Over-reaction and Under-reaction", ICFAI Journal of Behavioral Finance, 32-42.
27. R. D'Hulst and G.J.Rodgers (1999), "Exact Solution of a Model for Crowding and Information Transmission in Financial Markets", Vol.31.
28. Ian M Dobbs (1999), "The Anomaly of Size: Does It Really Matter?", *International Journal of Finance and Economics ,Int. J. Fin. Econ.* No. 4; 179–192.
29. Chiaku Chukwuogor-Ndu (2006), "Stock Market Returns Analysis, Day-of-the-Week Effect, Volatility of Returns: Evidence from European Financial Markets 1997-2004.", *International Research Journal of Finance and Economics,* Issue 1, Euro Journals Publishing, Inc.
30. Kenneth Ryack and Thomas Kida (2006), "Recall of Financial Information for Investment Decisions: The Impact of Encoding Specificity and Mental Imagery", *Journal of Behavioral Finance* Vol: 7, No: 4, 214-221.
31. Harry F. Griffin (2006), "Did Investor Sentiment Foretell the Fall of Enron?", *Journal of Behavioral Finance* , Vol: 7, No: 3, 26-127.
32. Erich Kirchler; Boris Maciejovsky and Martin Weber (2005), "Framing Effects, Selective Information, and Market Behavior: An Experimental Analysis", *Journal of Behavioral Finance,* Vol: 6, No: 2, 90-100.
33. Gokul Bhandari; Richard Deaves (2006), "The Demographics of Overconfidence", *Journal of Behavioral Finance,* Vol: 7, No: 1, 5-11.
34. Douglas Jordan; J. David Diltz (2004), "Day Traders and the Disposition Effect", *Journal of Behavioral Finance,* Vol: 5, No: 4, 192-200

35. Franco Caparelli; Anna Maria d'Arcangelis; Alexander Cassuto, (2004), "Herding in the Italian Stock Market: A Case of Behavioral Finance", *Journal of Behavioral Finance,* Vol: 5, No: 4, 222-230

36. Rank Westerhoff (2003), "Anchoring and Psychological Barriers in Foreign Exchange Markets", *Journal of Behavioral Finance,* Vol: 4, No: 2, 65-70.

37. David L. Schwarzkopf (2003), "The Effects of Attraction on Investment Decisions", *Journal of Behavioral Finance,* Vol: 4, No: 2, 96-108.

38. Aigbe Akhigbe; Stephen J.Larson; Jeff Madura (2002), "Market Underreaction and Overreaction of Technology Stocks", *Journal of Behavioral Finance,* Vol: 3, No: 3, 141-151.

39. Richard L. Peterson (2002), "Buy on the Rumor: Anticipatory Affect and Investor Behavior", *Journal of Behavioral Finance,* Vol: 3, No: 4, 218-226.

40. Tarek El-Sehity; Hans Haumer; Christian Helmenstein; Erich Kirchler; Boris Maciejovsky (2002), "Hindsight Bias and Individual Risk Attitude within the Context of Experimental Asset Markets", *Journal of Behavioral Finance,* Vol: 3, No: 4, 227-235.

41. Philip Y.K. Cheng (2007), "The Trader Interaction Effect on the Impact of Overconfidence on Trading Performance: An Empirical Study", *Journal of Behavioral Finance,* Vol: 8, No: 2, 59-69.

42. Malcolm Baker; Jeffrey Wurgler (2006), "Investor Sentiment and the Cross-section of Stock Returns", *Journal of Finance,* Vol: 61, No: 4, 1645-1680.

43. Andrea Frazzini (2006), "The Disposition Effect and Under-reaction to News", *Journal of Finance,* 61, No: 4, 2017-2046.

44. Alexander Ljungqvist and William J Wilhelm (2005), "Does Prospect Theory Explain IPO Market Behavior?", *Journal of Finance,* Vol: 60, No: 4, 1759-1790.

45. Kent D. Miller and Zur Shapira (2004), "An Empirical Test of Heuristics and Biases Affecting Real Option Valuation", *Strategic Management Journal,* No. 25 ; 269–284.

46. Jason Mitchell (2001), "Clustering and Psychological Barriers: The Importance of Numbers", *The Journal of Futures Markets,* Vol. 21, No. 5, 395–428.

47. John R. Nofsinger and Richard W. Sias (1999), "Herding and Feedback Trading by Institutional and Individual Investors", *The Journal of Finance*, Vol. LIV, No. 6.

48. Kent Daniel, David Hirshleifer and Avanidhar Subrahmanyam (1998), "Investor Psychology and Security Market Under-and Overreactions", *The Journal of Finance*, Vol. LIII, No. 6.

49. Imad A. Moosa (2007), "The Vanishing January Effect", *International Research Journal of Finance and Economics*, Issue 7.

50. Michael B. Clement and Senyo Y. Tse (2005), "Financial Analyst Characteristics and Herding Behavior in Forecasting", *The Journal of Finance*, Vol. LX, No. 1.

51. Alireza Tourani - Rad, Stephen Kirkby (2005), "Investigation of Investors' Overconfidence, Familiarity and Socialization", *Journal of Accounting and Finance*, 45, 283–300.

52. Allen M. Poteshman (2001), "Underreaction, Overreaction, and Increasing Misreaction to Information in the Options Market", *The Journal of Finance*, Vol. LVI, No. 3.

53. Balasingham Balachandran, Tuan Anh Nguyen (2004), "Signalling Power of Special Dividends in an Imputation Environment", *Journal of Accounting and Finance*, 44, 277–297.

54. George M. Constantinides (2002), "Rational Asset Prices", *The Journal of Finance* , Vol. Lvii, No. 4.

55. David R. Gallagher, Adrian Looi (2006), "Trading Behaviour and the Performance of Daily Institutional Trades", *Accounting and Finance*, 46, 125–147.

56. Werner Antweiler and Murray Z. Frank (2004), "Is All That Talk Just Noise? The Information Content of Internet Stock Message Boards", *The Journal of Finance*, Vol. Lix, No. 3.

57. Mahdi M. Hadi (2006), "Review of Capital Market Efficiency: Some Evidence from Jordanian Market", *International Research Journal of Finance and Economics*, Issue 3, 1450-2887.

58. Edwin J. Elton, Martin J. Gruber, and Jeffrey A. Busse (2004), "Are Investors Rational? Choices among Index Funds", *The Journal Of Finance*, Vol. Lix, No. 1.

59. David Hirshleifer (2001), "Investor Psychology and Asset Pricing", *The Journal of Finance*, Vol. Lvi, No. 4.

60. Joshua D. Coval and Tyler Shumway (2001), "Is Sound Just Noise?", *The Journal of Finance*, Vol. Lvi, No. 5.

61. Allenm Poteshmanandvitaly Serbin (2003), "Clearly Irrational Financial Market Behavior: Evidence from the Early Exercise of Exchange Traded Stock Options", *The Journal of Finance* , Vol. Lviii, No. 1.
62. Stefano Paleari and Silvio Vismara (2007), "Over-optimism when pricing IPOs", *Managerial Finance*, Vol. 33 No. 6, pp. 352-367.
63. Nicholas Barberis and Ming Huang (2001), "Mental Accounting, Loss Aversion, and Individual Stock Returns", *The Journal of Finance*, Vol. Lvi, No. 4.
64. Joshua D. Coval and Tyler Shumway (2005), "Do Behavioral Biases Affect Prices?", *The Journal of Finance*. Vol. Lx, No. 1.
65. Harrison Hong and Jeremy C. Stein (1999), "A Unified Theory of Underreaction, Momentum Trading, and Overreaction in Asset Markets', *The Journal of Finance*, Vol. Liv, No. 6.
66. Mark Grinblatt and Matti Keloharju (2001), "What Makes Investors Trade?", *The Journal of Finance*, Vol. Lvi, No. 2.
67. Gordon Gemmill and Dylan C. Thomas (2002), "Noise Trading, Costly Arbitrage, and Asset Prices: Evidence from Closed-end Funds", *The Journal of Finance*, Vol. Lvii, No. 6.
68. Michael F. Fergusonand, Richard L. Shockleyn (2003), "Equilibrium''Anomalies'', *The Journal of Finance*, Vol. Lviii, No. 6.
69. David Michayluk, Karyn L. Neuhauser (2006), "Investor Overreaction During Market Declines: Evidence from the 1997 Asian Financial Crisis", *The Journal of Financial Research*, Vol. XXIX, No. 2, 217–234.
70. Leonid Kogan, Stephen A. Ross, Jiang Wang and Mark M. Westerfield (2006), "The Price Impact and Survival of Irrational Traders", *The Journal of Finance*, Vol. Lxi, No. 1,
71. Chiaku Chukwuogor–Ndu (2006), "Stock Market Returns Analysis, Day-of-the-Week Effect, Volatility of Returns: Evidence from European Financial Markets 1997-2004.", *International Research Journal of Finance and Economics*,1450-2887 Issue 1.
72. Alexander Ljungqvist and William J. Wilhelm, Jr. (2005), "Does Prospect Theory Explain IPO Market Behavior?", *The Journal of Finance*, Vol. Lx, No. 4.
73. Statman, Meir (1987), "How Many Stocks Make a Diversified Portfolio?" *Journal of Financial and Quantitative Analysis*, 22.

Footnotes

i. Heuristic : enabling one to learn or discover something for themselves. In problem solving situations, it refers to "rules of thumb" that allows to factor a complex situation into simple component, reducing the search in problem-solving activities.

ii. Irrational Exuberance : a phrase used by former Federal Reserve Board Chairman Alan Greenspan in a speech given at the American Enterprise Institute during the stock market boom of the 1990s interpreting, a heightened state of speculative fervor.

iii. Bubble crash : a self-perpetuating rise or boom in the share prices of stocks of a particular industry. The term is used in retrospect, when share prices have since crashed. A bubbie occurs when speculators note the fast increase in value and decide to buy in anticipation of further rises. Typically many companies thus become grossly overvalued. When the bubble "bursts," the share prices fall dramatically, and many companies go out of business.

iv. Herding Behavior : follow the mass without applying the mind

v. Anchoring or focalism is a *cognitive bias* that describes the common human tendency to rely too heavily, or "anchor," on a piece of information when making decisions. According to this heuristic, people start with an implicitly suggested reference point (the "anchor") and make adjustments to it to reach their estimate.

4

Personal Factors and Investment Profile of Investors

Investments in capital market, are based on decisions, to choose the right stocks and these decisions preludes, the answers to some basic questions like; How much money to invest? What type of investment return is expected to be achieved? How much risk the investor is willing to take? The basic proposition being greater the risk higher the returns, but cannot deny the fact that it might lead to heavy losses also. How much risk to be taken with the money invested depends on many different factors such as age, risk tolerance, and investment objectives. No matter where the money is invested, it is a prerogative to understand the various types of risks involved and their potential rewards.

Thus it can be said that the Investors' behavioral intentions and decisions in selection of right Investment Portfolio, is based on a host of factors, both personal and investment factors, included in the questionnaire for analysis A few of them are ; Age, occupational category, educational level and period of investment etc., appears to have a profound effect on the investor's behavioral patterns and the investment in the stock market. This chapter attempts to analyse the above issues, portrayed under the following headings:

(a) Age of the respondent Investors

(b) Educational Qualification of the Respondents

(c) Occupational category of the Respondents

(d) Experience of the Respondents

(e) Tenure of Investment

(f) Investment Allocation

(g) Investment Category

(h) Current Value of Investment

(i) Basis for Choice of Investment

(j) Basic Nature of Investors

(k) Reasons to Avoid in Investment

(l) Expected Rate of Return

(m) Average Earned Return

(n) Basis for Investment Decision

(o) Justification for Investment Decision

The data collected for the question numbers 2 to 16 pertaining to the personal factors and including the Investment profile of the investors such as the Value of Investment made, Investor Category they belong, their Expected and Average Earned Return on investment, Basis for investment decisions and Reasons for justifying their decisions, of the questionnaire (Refer Appendix 1), from the respondents has been analysed. The method of examination used were, frequency distribution and percentage analysis to explain the personal profile and investment factors.

Table 1
Age Wise Distribution of the Respondents

Age (years)	*Frequency*	*Percent*	*Cumulative Percent*
20- 30	79	26.3	26.3
30 - 40	28	9.4	35.7
40 - 50	102	34.0	69.7
50 and Above	91	30.3	100.0
Total	300	100.0	

Some of the important factors like Age, Education, Occupational category, Tenure of investment, Experience, Value of Investment, has been compared with the Basic Nature of Investors categorized as Risk Averse, Risk Neutral and Risk Takers, applying the Correlation and Chi-square test, to project the relationship of their personal factors with their risk taking capacity.

In the above Table No. 1, nearly one-third of the investors ie., 34 percent are in the age group of 40 and 50, and 30 percent of them are above the age of 50, followed by the respondents within the age group of 20-30 years and 30-40 years, having 26.3 percent and 9.3 percent respectively. The investors above the age of 40 years fall under the earning category, from the industry, Business entrepreneurs, professionals including retired people. The same results are depicted in Figure 1.

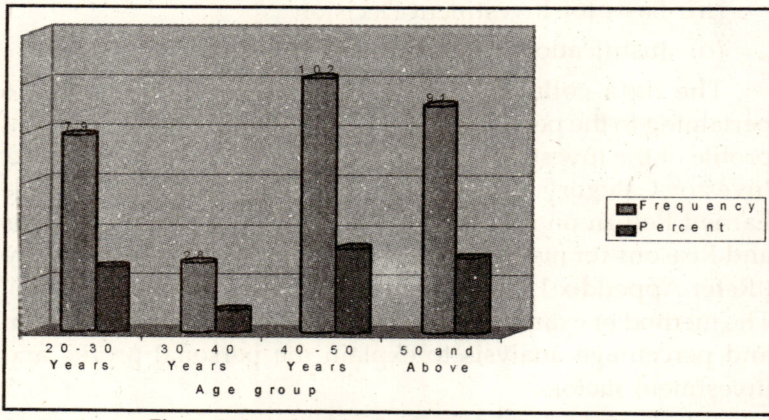

Figure 1: Agewise Distribution of the Respondents

Table 2
Educational Qualification of the Respondents

Education	*Frequency*	*Percent*	*Cumulative Percent*
Secondary	21	7.0	7.0
H. Secondary	19	6.3	13.3
Graduate	76	25.3	38.7
Post graduate	104	34.7	73.3
Professional	80	26.7	100.0
Total	300	100.0	

The educational qualification of the respondents shown in Table No. 2, depicts 34.7 percent being post-graduates, 26.7

percent caters to investors having Professional Education, followed by 25.3 percent being graduates. Remaining 13 percent are in the secondary or higher secondary category. Education has a major impact in capital market investments, were most of the respondents seem to be well educated, showing much interest in the stock market. The information in Table No.2 has been shown as a graphical representation in Fig. 2.

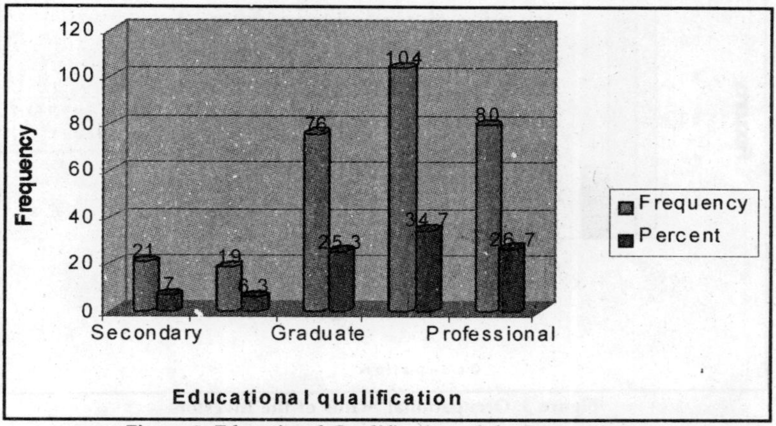

Figure 2: Educational Qualification of the Respondents

Table 3
Distribution of Investors Based on Occupational Status

Occupational Status of the Investors	*Frequency*	*Percent*	*Cumulative Percent*
Private	114	38.0	38.0
Public	47	15.7	53.7
Self-Employed	39	13.0	66.7
Business	30	10.0	76.7
Student/Learner	46	15.3	92.0
Others	24	8.0	100.0
Total	300	100.0	

In the above Table No. 3, more than one-third of the respondents belong to those working in Private firms, followed by 15.7 percent ie., one-sixth of them, are from the Public concerns. The students take a share of 15.3 percent of the total respondents. This indicates the increased awareness and interest, among the youth towards investment in capital market. Those in business and self-employed have a share of ten and thirteen percent only. This can be associated with the deployment of funds required for Business sustenance and growth. The data in Table 3 has been shown as the graphical representation in Fig. 3.

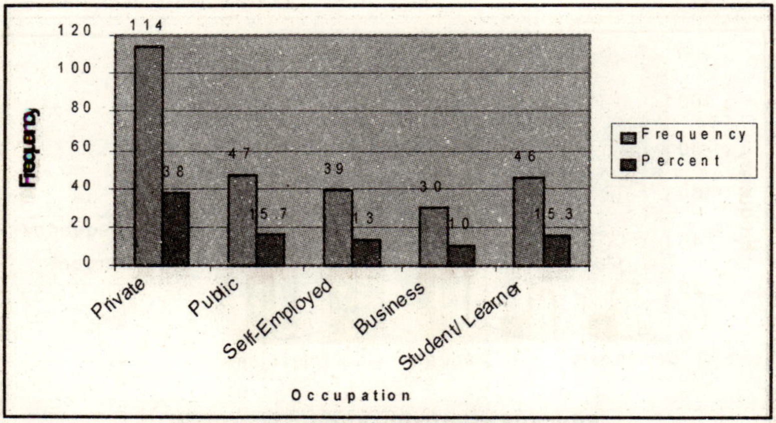

Figure 3: Occupational Status of the Investors

Table 4
Experience of the Respondents

Experience	*Frequency*	*Percent*	*Cumulative Percent*
< 5 years	111	37.0	37.0
5 – 10 years	65	21.7	58.7
10 – 15 years	57	19.0	77.7
> 15 years	67	22.3	100.0
Total	300	100.0	

Table No. 4 shows that more than one-third of the respondents, ie., 37 percent are those having less than 5 years of experience in the capital market. This indicates the increased awareness and inclination towards capital market in recent years. Followed by 21.7 percent having an experience of 5-10 years and 22.3 percent possess more than 15 years of experience. The remaining 19 percent of them, have an experience between 10 and 15 years. This is depicted in Figure 4.

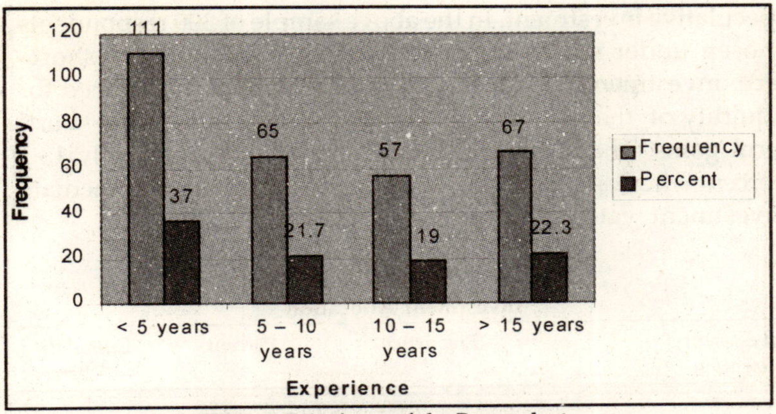

Figure 4: Experience of the Respondents

Table 5
Tenure of Investment

Tenure	*Frequency*	*Percent*	*Cumulative Percent*
Long term	41	13.7	13.7
Intermediate	11	3.6	17.3
Short term	188	62.7	80.0
Speculative	60	20.0	100.0
Total	300	100.0	

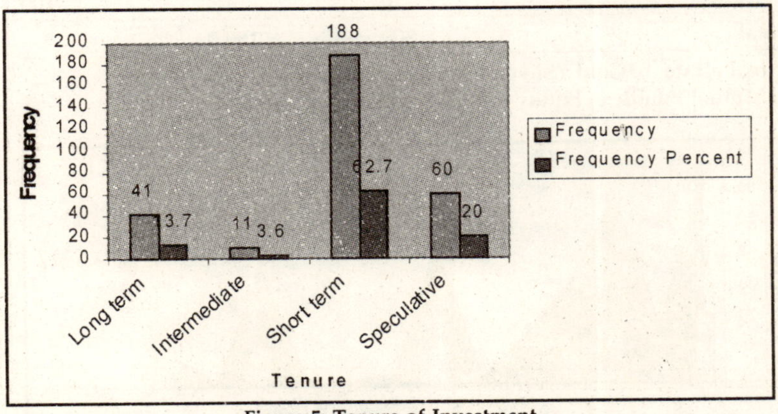

Figure 5: Tenure of Investment

The above frequency Table No. 5, shows a highest 62.7 percent of short–term investment followed by 20 percent of speculative investment. In the above sample of 300 respondents chosen under study, majority of them had opted for short–term investment. This behavioral pattern, depicts the need for liquidity of the investments made as also of immediate short-term gains. The long-term investment stands to be only 13.7 percent whereas a meagre 3.6 percent, where in the intermediate investment category. The same is depicted in Figure 5.

Table 6
Investment Allocation

Investment Allocation	*Frequency*	*Percent*	*Cumulative Percent*
a,e	66	22	22
b,e	19	6	28
c,e	59	20	48
d,e	33	11	59
a,b,e	16	5	64
a,c,e	3	1	65
a,d,e	45	15	80
b,d,e	4	1	81
c,d,e	2	1	82
a,b,c,e	3	1	83
a,b,d,e	38	13	96
a,c,d,e	2	1	97
a,b,c,d,e	10	3	100
Total	300	100.0	

a. real estate b. Gold /Silver c. Consumer durables
d. Mutual Funds e. Equity/Bonds/Debentures

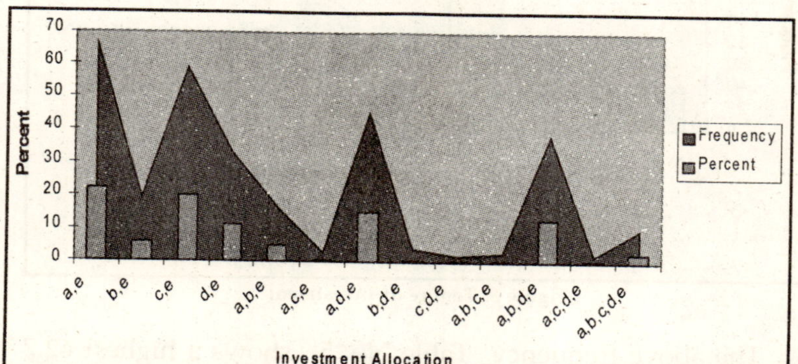

Figure 6: Investment Allocation

The choice on allocation of investment as shown in Table 6, on physical and financial assets by the respondents has revealed, invariably, their interest on stock market investment. A certain proportion of their surplus income is contributed for purchase of equity/bonds/debentures. Ten percent of the investors have a combination of all types of assets. The data on the allocation of investment is shown in Figure 6.

Table 7
Investor Category

Investor Category	*Frequency*	*Percent*	*Cumulative Percent*
Fund Managers	9	3.0	3.0
HNIs	24	8.0	11.0
Retail Investors	216	72.0	83.0
Intermediary investors	51	17.0	100.0
Total	300	100.0	

From the above Table No. 7, out of 300 respondents, three-fourth of them are retail investors. Followed by 17 percent being intermediary investors, 8 percent are HNIs (High Networth Individuals), and 3 percent caters to Institutional Investors. The retail investors constitute, short-term, medium and long-term investors whose quantum of investment is much lesser than the other Investor category. The Size of investment of HNIs, and Institutional investors are normally huge, ranging more than 50 lakhs at a stroke. The Institutional Investments

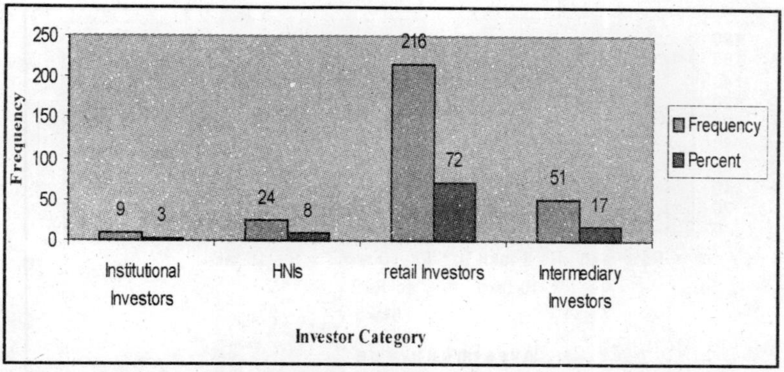

Figure 7: Investor Category

pertains to mainly Mutual Funds and Domestic Financial Institutions (DFIs) and FIIs (Foreign Institutional Investments). The Intermediary investors include the traders, stock brokers and persons providing PMS (Portfolio Management Services), who buy and sell securities on their own account or/and on account of their clients. The data in Table 7 has been depicted in Figure 7.

Table 8
Current Value of Investment

Investment Value	*Frequency*	*Percent*	*Cumulative Percent*
< Rs.500000	167	55.7	55.7
Rs.500000 to 1000000	98	32.7	88.3
Rs.1000000 to Rs. 1500000	10	3.3	91.7
> Rs.1500000	25	8.3	100.0
Total	300	100.0	

The above Table No. 8 shows that more than half of the respondents ie., 55.7 percent of the investors have a total value of investment less than Rs. 5,00,000, followed by 32.7 percent of them have made an investment of Rs. 5 lakh to 10 lakh. A minimum of 8.3 percent of the investors, have a contribution of more than Rs. 15 lakh and the remaining 3.3 percent range between Rs. 10 lakh and Rs. 15 lakh. The same has been shown in Figure 8.

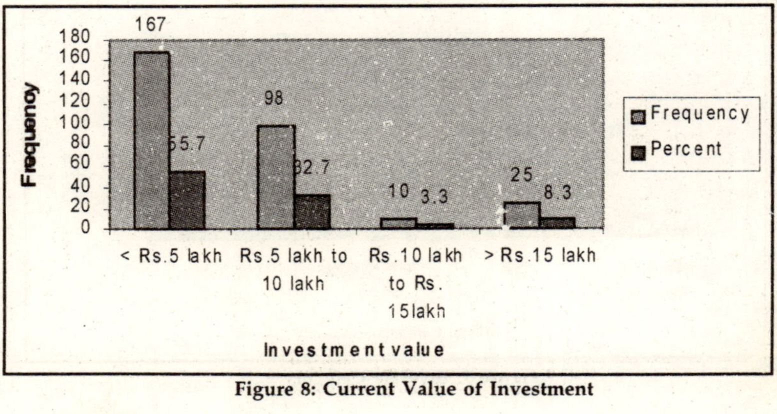

Figure 8: Current Value of Investment

Table 9
Basis for Choice of Investment

Basis for Choice of Investment	*Frequency*	*Percent*	*Cumulative Percent*
A	101	33.7	33.7
B	11	3.7	37.3
C	25	8.3	45.7
D	119	39.7	85.3
a & c	10	3.3	88.7
a & d	27	9.0	97.7
b & c	1	.3	98.0
b & d	1	.3	98.3
a & c & d	5	1.7	100.0
Total	300	100.0	

a. Industry b. Religion c. Management team d. Market Reaction

Any investment in stock market preludes on various choices. A few of such choices of investment will be based on the image of the organization having an impact on the management team which leads the organization. Table No. 9 shows the data relating to the basis for choice of investment. The choice can be based on Industry preferences or blindly based on the market reaction related to the performance of a particular industry or company/s, which is aligned with the corporate news and deliberate announcements made through the media. Rarely, the investment choices can also be influenced based on the religion they are associated with.

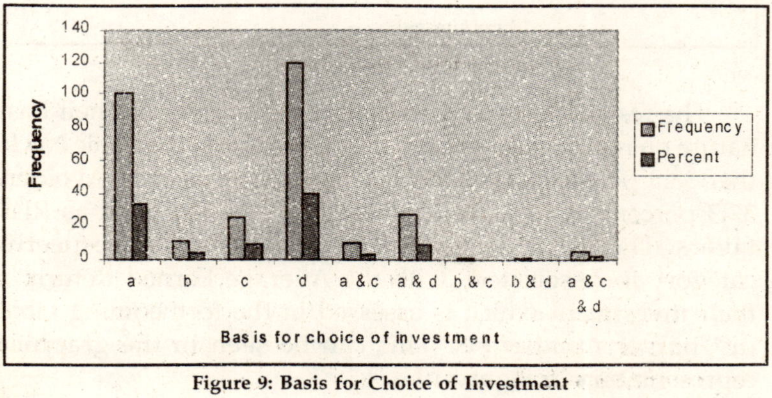

Figure 9: Basis for Choice of Investment

The study has revealed that majority of the respondents ie., 39.7 percent and 33.7 percent, of the investor's choice is based on the Market reaction and Industry based choice. The investors seem to have much affinity towards the market information, more inclined to the decisions of the market participants and also the investment choice is much of Industry based. This has been shown in Figure 9.

Table10
Type of Investors

Type of Investors	*Frequency*	*Percent*	*Cumulative Percent*
Risk Averse	100	33.3	33.3
Risk Neutral	112	37.3	70.7
Risk Takers	88	29.3	100.0
Total	300	100.0	

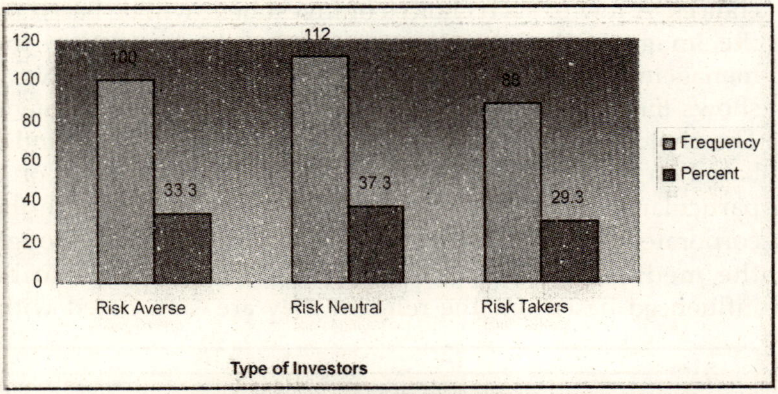

Figure10: Type of Investors

The respondents have identified themselves on their basic nature on risk taking capacity. It is found from the Table No.10, that 33.3 percent have labelled themselves as Risk Avoiders, 37.3 percent as Risk-Neutral and only 29.3 percent as Risk-takers. The identification of themselves in the respective category is associated with the Average Earned Return on their investment which is assessed in the forthcoming tables in Chapter number six. This can be seen in the graphical representation in Figure 10.

Table 11
Reasons to Avoid in Investment

Reasons to Avoid Investment	*Frequency*	*Percent*	*Cumulative Percent*
a	15	5.0	5.0
b	47	15.7	20.7
c	105	35.0	55.7
d	133	44.3	100.0
Total	300	100.0	

a. Not owning the best performing types of investment
b. Don't depend on either fundamental/Technical analysis
c. Trust only on my intuition.
d. Over-react to the fears of uncertain times/euphoria of good times

From the above Table No. 11, 44.3 percent of the respondents has suggested that they would prefer to avoid over-reacting to the fears of uncertain times or euphoria of good times, 35 percent preferred to avoid decisions trusting only on their intuitions, 15.7 percent try to avoid not to depend on fundamental and technical analysis, and 5 percent prefer to own the best performing types of investment. The data pertaining to reasons to avoid in investment has been depicted in Figure 11.

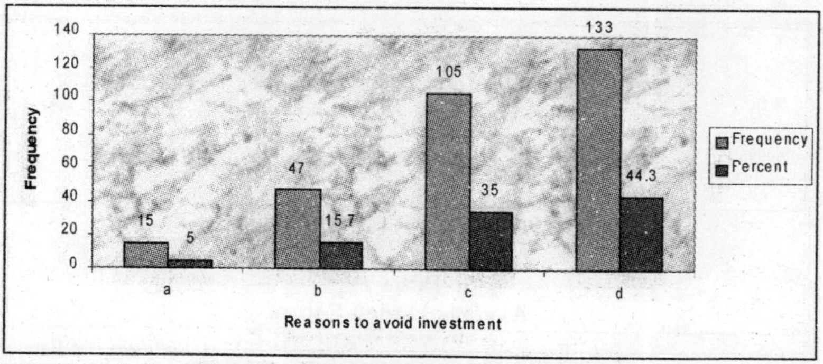

Figure 11: Reasons to Avoid in Investment

The Expected Rate of Return on Investment of all respondents are relatively higher than their Actual Earned Return. The above Table No. 12, reveals that all the investors expectation on the return from stock market is much higher.

58.3 percent of the respondents expect that their returns would be greater than 50 percent. 18.7 percent of the respondents expected a return of 20 percent to 30 percent, 13.3 percent have expected a return of 40 percent to 50 percent and only 1.7 percent of them have expected a return of less than 20 percent. This is shown in Figure 12.

Table 12
Expected Rate of Return

ERR	*Frequency*	*Percent*	*Cumulative Percent*
> 50 %	175	58.3	58.3
50% to 40%	40	13.3	71.7
40% to 30%	24	8.0	79.7
30% to 20%	56	18.7	98.3
< 20 %	5	1.7	100.0
Total	300	100.0	

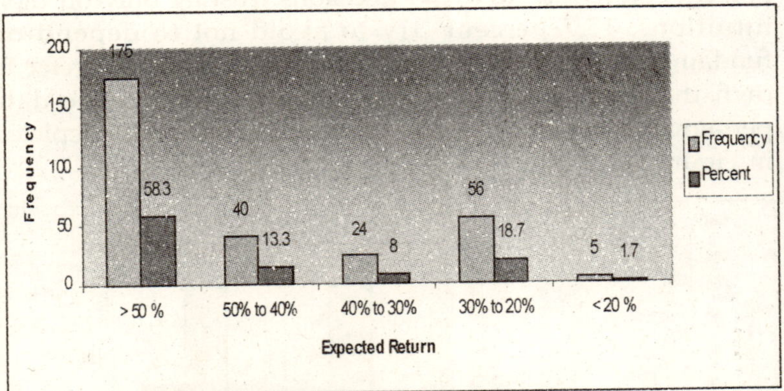

Figure 12: Expected Rate of Return

Table 13
Average Earned Return

AER	*Frequency*	*Percent*	*Cumulative Percent*
> 40 %	53	17.7	17.7
30% to 40%	79	26.3	44.0
20% to 30%	99	33.0	77.0
10% to 20%	34	11.3	88.3
10% to -10%	35	11.7	100.0
Total	300	100.0	

Comparing with the Expected Return, the above Table No. 13, shows that 33 percent of the respondents have an Actual Earned Return of 20 percent to 30 percent, 26.3 percent of them have earned a return of 30 percent to 40 percent, 17.7 percent have Earned Returns above 40 percent, 11.7 percent have earned less than 10 percent to losses sustained upto 10% and 11.3 percent have earned a return of 10 percent to 20 percent.

Table 14
Basis for Investment Decision

Basis for Investment Decision	*Frequency*	*Percent*	*Cumulative Percent*
Sole decision	210	70.0	70.0
Peer/friend's opinion	67	22.3	92.3
Family/spouse opinion	23	7.7	100.0
Total	300	100.0	

The Investors in stock market generally decide on their investments based on various factors. Investment in stock market involves huge risk, requiring a strong mental ability to accept the risk of losses. In the above Table No. 14, around

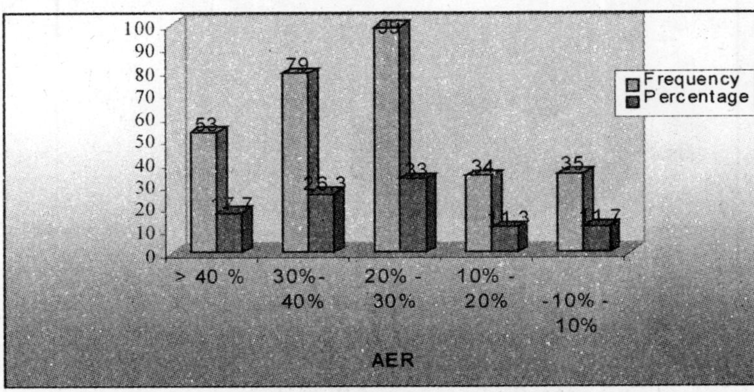

Figure 13: Average Earned Return

70 percent of the Investors have opined that they take decisions individually on their own, 22.3 percent have suggested that they take the opinion of their friends and peer group , and 7.7 percent have agreed that they would take the suggestions of

their family and spouse. The decisions are normally biased since human beings' attitude of Loss Aversion is much greater than the loss itself, Kahneman and Tversky (1979) and Tversky and Kahneman (1992). Hence further analysis is required to conclude, which category of the investors decisions are influenced by suggestions, either sole or peer or family. The data has been represented graphically in Figure 14.

Table 15
Justification for Investment Decision

Justification for Investment Decision	*Frequency*	*Percent*	*Cumulative Percent*
a	119	39.7	39.7
b	54	18.0	57.7
c	127	42.3	100.0
Total	300	100.0	

a. My instinct based on market movements
b. Technical Analysis made by myself
c. Advice taken from technical analyst

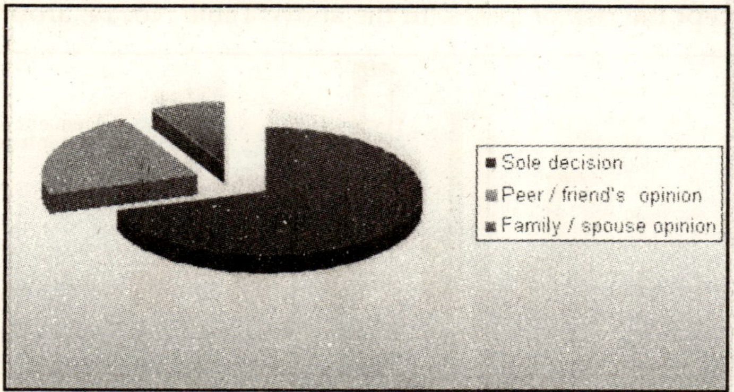

Figure14: Basis for Investment Decision

Investors normally tend to get the advice from the analysts or some might take intuitive decisions. In the above Table 15, around 42.3 percent have suggested that they take the advice from the technical analysts, 39.7 percent have taken decisions based on their intuitions and 18 percent have taken decisions based on their own self–analysis. This is shown in Figure 15.

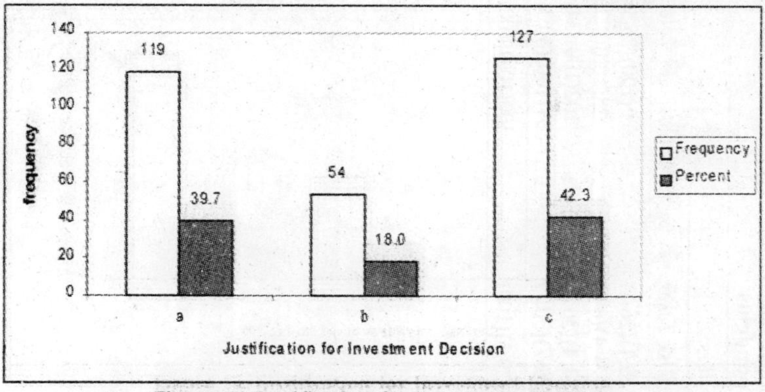

Figure 15: Justification for Investment Decision

The frequency percentage analysis, is extended with further analysis applying the chi-square test to each variable against the Type of investors to assess the existence of significant relationship between the constant variable (ie., Type of Investors), and the other related variables such as Age of respondents, Educational qualification of respondents, Occupational category, Tenure of Investment, Investment value, Expected Returns, and Basis for Investment Decisions.

Analysis and Discussion

The following null hypothesis are developed to examine the Nature of investors with their personal and investment factors.

H_1 : There is no relationship between the personal factors and the investors' risk-taking capacity.

H_2 : The investment profile of the investors does not have any relationship with the Investors' risk-taking capacity.

The data pertaining to the relationship between the personal factors and the investors' risk-taking capacity of the sample are presented in Table No. 16.

Several studies have classified the investors broadly as Risk Takers, Risk Averse and Risk Neutral. The respondents have done a self-assessment on themselves under each one of the three categories they belong to. Taking their Age factor as an independent variable, a correlation analysis is made with the

Table 16

Association between Nature of Investors and Age of Respondents

Age of the Respondents	*Basic Nature of Investors*			*Total*
	Risk Averse	*Risk Neutral*	*Risk Taker*	
20- 30 Years	49(62)(49)	7(8.9)(6.3)	23(29.1)(26.1)	79(100)(26.3)
30 - 40 Years	6(21.4)(6)	16(57.1)(14.3)	6(21.4)(6.8)	28(100)(9.3)
40 - 50 Years	7(6.9)(7)	63(61.8)(56.3)	32(31.4)(36.4)	102(100)(34)
50 and Above	38(41.8)(38)	26(28.6)(23.2)	27(29.7)(30.7)	91(100)(30.3)
Total	100(33.3)(100)	112(37.3)(100)	88(29.3)(100)	300(100)(100)

Source Question No. 10 and 1 of the Questionnaire

nature of investors. It is found from the above Table No. 16, that majority of the respondents ie., 62 percent, within the age of 20 to 30 years and 41.8 percent in the age group of above 50 years are Risk Avoiders. In the Risk Neutral category, 61.8 percent, followed by 57 percent, are within the age of 40 to 50 years and 30 to 40 years. Nearly one-third of the respondents within the age of 40 and above and 20 to 30 years are found to be Risk-Takers.

Finally, from the data analysis, it can be said, that Risk Takers are more in number, in the age group of 40 and above and risk-Avoiders seem to be high within the age group of 20 to 30 years. Therefore it can be concluded that, higher the age, greater the risk taken whereas lesser the age, the risk taking capacity is low.

Table 17
Pearson's Value

		Value	*Asymp. Std. Error*	*Approx. T*	*Approx. Sig.*
Nominal by Nominal	Contingency Coefficient	.466			.000
Interval by Interval	Pearson's R	.135	.064	2.352	.019
N of Valid Cases			300		

Source: Output of SPSS

From Table No. 17 it could be seen that the pearson's correlation r value is very insignificant showing a low positive relationship between nature of investors and their age. Hence it may be concluded that the risk takers of all categories are spread over in all age groups.

It is observed from the Table 18, majority of the respondents, ie., more than 75 percent of Post graduates and Professionals are risk neutral, who, neither avoid risk or affected by a loss on risk. Less than One-fourth of the Professionals observed to be Risk-Takers and Risk Averse.

Majority of the respondents qualified as Post-Graduates seem to be risk Takers (42%) and Professionals are observed

Table 18

Association between Nature of Investors and Educational Qualification of the Respondents

		Basic Nature of Investors			
		Risk Averse	*Risk Neutral*	*Risk Taker*	*Total*
Educational Qualification of the Respondents	secondary	2(9.5)(2)	1(4.8)(0.9)	18(85.7)(20.5)	21(100)(7)
	H. Secondary	16(84.2)(16)	3(15.8)(2.7)	0(0)(0)	19(100)(6.3)
	graduate	39(51.3)(39)	19(25)(17)	18(23.7)(20.5)	76(100)(25.3)
	post graduate	23(22.1)(23)	47(45.2)(42)	34(32.7)(38.6)	104(100)(34.7)
	professional	20(25)(20)	42(52.5)(37.5)	18(22.5)(20.5)	80(100)(26.7)
Total		100(33.3)(100)	112(37.3)(100)	88(29.3)(100)	300(100)(100)

Source: Question No. 10 and 2 of the Questionnaire

to be Risk-Neutral (37.5%). It can be concluded that more qualified tend to be objective in taking decisions. Less educated (84.2%) were found to be Risk-Avoiders.

Table No. 19 reveals the X^2 (Chi-square) test results pertaining to Nature of Investors and Educational Qualification of respondents.

Table 19
Chi-Square Test

	Value	*df*	*Asymp. Sig. (2-sided)*
Pearson Chi-Square	80.199	8	.000
Likelihood Ratio	78.719	8	.000
Linear-by-Linear Association	.003	1	.955
N of Valid Cases	300		

Source: Output of SPSS

The above chi-square test reveals a significance level of .000. Since the level of significance is less than 0.05 it is concluded that there exists relationship between the two variables, Nature of Investors and their Educational qualification.

The Table 20, shows that Majority of those working in private concerns are observed from the data to be Risk takers. Nearly 40 percent of the students were Risk-Avoiders. The respondents who were Risk-Neutral were more or less the same among those from private, public, business and self-employed. Hence, from the data it is concluded that the students were cautious in taking decisions and tried to avoid risk to the maximum possible. Those working in private concerns, are found to be capable of taking higher risk in capital market investments. And those who were in business and self-employed entrepreneurs, were observed to be risk-neutral.

Since the level of significance value is less than .05, from the Table 21 above it is concluded that there is significant relationship between the two variables, Nature of Investors and occupation category they belong to.

The data relating to cross correlation between Nature of Investors and Experience of the respondents are presented in Table 22.

Table 20

Association between Nature of Investors and Occupational Status of the Respondents

		Basic Nature of Investors			
		Risk Averse	*Risk Neutral*	*Risk Taker*	*Total*
Occupational Status of the Respondents	private	23(20.2)(23)	24(21.1)(21.4)	67(58.8)(76.1)	114(100)(38)
	public	12(25.5)(12)	28(59.6)(25)	7(14.9)(8)	47(100)(15.7)
	self employed	15(38.5)(15)	19(48.7)(17)	5(12.8)(5.7)	39(100)(13)
	Business	4(13.3)(4)	23(76.7)(20.5)	3(10)(3.4)	30(100)(10)
	students	41(89.1)(41)	2(4.3)(1.8)	3(6.5)(3.4)	46(100)(15.3)
	others	5(20.8)(5)	16(66.7)(14.3)	3(12.5)(3.4)	24(100)(8)
Total		100(33.3)(100)	112(37.3)(100)	88(29.3)(100)	300(100)(100)

Source: Question No. 10 and 3 of the Questionnaire

Table 21
Chi-Square Test

	Value	*df*	*Asymp. Sig. (2-sided)*
Pearson Chi-Square	156.769(a)	10	.000
Likelihood Ratio	150.020	10	.000
Linear-by-Linear Association	50.124	1	.000
N of Valid Cases	300		

Source: Output of SPSS

The data from the Table No. 22, reveals that 42 percent of the Risk-Takers were having an investment experience between 10 to 15 years followed by those having less than 5 years. More than 60 percent of the respondents having less than 5 years experience were observed to be Risk-Averse. Nearly half the respondents having greater than 15 years experience were found to be Risk-Neutral.

It can be concluded from the data that higher the Experience, greater is the Risk Tolerance and become Risk Neutral due to their longer association with capital Market. The new entrants having lesser experience about the nuances of the capital market are prone to be Risk-Avciders. Those within a medium term period of association are found to be Risk Takers.

From the Table No. 23, it is to be noticed that the calculated value of chi-square is .000 (Pearson's), which is less than the hypothetical value (=0.05) at 5% significance level. Therefore the null hypothesis is not accepted. Hence concluded that there is a significant relationship between the two variables, Nature of investors and experience gained by the investors in stock market investments.

The Investors before deciding to enter the Capital market pre-decide the tenure of their investment. Normally the Retail Investors tend to choose long-term investment for the purpose of reaping capital gains and earn stable returns. The Institutional Investors constitute Mutual Fund and Portfolio Managers, who opt for either short term or medium term of investment. For deciding the tenure, some of the major factors like safety and liquidity of Investment play a dominant or a lead role prior to quick or exorbitant returns.

Table 22

Association between Nature of Investors and Experience of the Respondents

		Basic Nature of Investors			
		Risk Averse	*Risk Neutral*	*Risk Taker*	*Total*
Experience of the Respondents	< 5 years	67(60.4)(67)	17(15.3)(15.2)	27(24.3)(30.7)	111(100)(37)
	5 to 10 years	25(38.5)(25)	25(38.5)(22.3)	15(23.1)(17)	65(100)(21.7)
	10 to 15 years	2(3.5)(2)	18(31.6)(16)	37(64.9)(42)	57(100)(19)
	> 15 years	6(9)(6)	52(77.6)(46.4)	9(13.4)(10.2)	67(100)(22.3)
Total	100(33.3)(100)	112(37.3)(100)	88(29.3)(100)	300(100)(100)	

Source: Question No. 10 and 4 of the Questionnaire

Table 23
Chi-Square Test

	Value	df	Asymp. Sig. (2-sided)
Pearson Chi-Square	128.240(a)	6	.000
Likelihood Ratio	130.634	6	.000
Linear-by-Linear Association	27.261	1	.000
N of Valid Cases	300		

Table 24
Association between Nature of Investors and Tenure of Investment

		Basic Nature of Investors			
		Risk Averse	Risk Neutral	Risk Taker	Total
Tenure of Investment	long term	14(34.1)(14)	15(36.6)(13.4)	12(29.3)(13.6)	41(100)(13.7)
	intermediate	5(45.5)(5)	3(27.3)(2.7)	3(27.3)(3.4)	11(100)(3.7)
	short term	60(31.9)(60)	59(31.4)(52.7)	69(36.7)(78.4)	188(100)(62.7)
	speculative	21(35)(21)	35(58.3)(31.3)	4(6.7)(4.5)	60(100)(20)
Total		100(33.3)(100)	112(37.3)(100)	88(29.3)(100)	300(100)(100)

Source Question No. 10 and 5 of the Questionnaire

The Table No. 24 shows that short- term investors have a higher Risk-Taking ability than others. One-third of the speculative investors who are more inclined towards day-trading with an urge of earning immediate gains are observed to be Risk-Neutral. This attitude can be due to their experience facing both the losses and gains in day-to day basis, making them immune to risk. One–fourth of the speculative investors seem to be Risk Avoiders also. Hence, can be concluded from the data that short-term investors take higher risk and speculative investors are found to be more or less the same between both Risk-Neutral and Risk-Averse.

Table 25
Chi-Square Test

	Value	df	Asymp. Sig. (2-sided)
Pearson Chi-Square	23.836(a)	6	.001
Likelihood Ratio	27.453	6	.000
Linear-by-Linear Association	1.046	1	.306
N of Valid Cases	300		

Source: Output of SPSS

Table 26

Association between Nature of Investors and Value of Investment

		Basic Nature of Investors			
		Risk Averse	*Risk Neutral*	*Risk Taker*	*Total*
Current Value of Investment	< Rs. 5 lakh	68(40.7)(68)	44(26.3)(39.3)	55(32.9)(62.5)	167(100)(55.7)
	Rs. 5 lakh to Rs.10 lakh	30(30.6)(30)	38(38.8)(33.9)	30(30.6)(34.1)	98(100)(32.7)
	Rs.10 lakh to Rs. 15 lakh	2(20)(2)	7(70)(6.3)	1(10)(1.1)	10(100)(3.3)
	> Rs.15 lakh	0(0)(0)	23(92)(20.5)	2(8)(2.3)	25(100)(8.3)
Total		100(33.3)(100)	112(37.3)(100)	88(29.3)(100)	300(100)(100)

Source: Question No. 10 and 8 of the Questionnaire

From the Table No. 25, the significance value is found to be less than .05, Hence concluded that there is a significant relationship between the two variables, Nature of investors and Tenure of investment chosen by the investors in their stock market investments.

In Table No. 26, more than 60 percent of those investors with a value of investment, less than Rs.5 lakh found to be Risk Averse and Risk Takers. One–third of the respondents with an investment of Rs. 5 lakh to Rs.15 lakh were observed to be more or less the same in all three categories.s. Those who have invested more than Rs. 15 lakh, were found to be Risk Neutral. Such large investments are normally from the Institutional Investors or HNIs, hence, it can be concluded that, they are neither Risk Takers, who generally prefer investments in blue chip companies, nor they avoid risk. The investors with less value of investment, are small investors, who try to avoid taking risk and the other category of investors, intend to take more risk due to greediness of earning immediate profits.

Table 27
Chi-Square Test

	Value	*df*	*Asymp. Sig. (2-sided)*
Pearson Chi-Square	46.086(a)	6	.000
Likelihood Ratio	50.511	6	.000
Linear-by-Linear Association	.917	1	.338
N of Valid Cases	300		

Source: Output of SPSS

Since the significance value from the Table No. 27, is found to be less than .05, it is concluded that there is a significant relationship between the two variables, Nature of investors and the Value of investment made by the investors.

Decisions vary from person to person, especially in capital market investments. The decisions are based on the nature of investors which are sometimes influenced by the peer group or suggestions given by friends and preferences by spouse or family members. Some of the investors having more of intuitiveness and the day traders with more of gut feeling tend to take decisions and act on their own instincts. From the Table No. 28, more than 75 percent of the Risk Takers react on sole decisions, 70 percent of Risk Averse people tend to take decisions on their own as also 60 percent of the Risk neutral investors. Those in all three categories are of minimal percentage, who act on decisions given by family members. But one-fourth of all the categories tend to take advice from their friends and peer group.

Table 28
Association between Nature of Investors and Basis for Investment Decision

		Basic Nature of Investors			
		Risk Averse	*Risk Neutral*	*Risk Taker*	*Total*
Basis for Investment Decision	sole decision	72(34.3)(72)	68(32.4)(60.7)	70(33.3)(79.5)	210(100)(70)
	peer/friend's opinion	24(35.8)(24)	28(41.8)(25)	15(22.4)(17)	67(100)(22.3)
	family/spouse opinion	4(17.4)(4)	16(69.6)(14.3)	3(13)(3.4)	23(100)(7.7)
Total		100(33.3)(100)	112(37.3)(100)	88(29.3)(100)	300(100)(100)

Source: Question No. 10 and 14 of the Questionnaire

Table 29
Chi Square Test

Value	*df*		*Asymp. Sig. (2-sided)*
Pearson Chi-Square	14.400	4	.006
Likelihood Ratio	14.112	4	.007
Linear-by-Linear Association	.575	1	.448
N of Valid Cases	300		

Source: Output of SPSS

From the Table No. 29, the significance value is found to be more than .05, only with a marginal difference of .01, Hence it can be concluded that there is a significant relationship between the two variables, Nature of investors and the Basis of investment decisions taken by the investors in their stock market investments.

Table No. 30 reveals, Majority of the retail investors were found to be Risk Averse and around 60 percent of retail investors were found to be both Risk Takers and Risk Neutral.

The intermediary investors are more or less the same in all three categories. The Fund Managers were more in Risk Taking category. Majority of the HNIs were found to be Risk Neutral.

Table 30
Association between Investor Category and Nature of Investors

		Basic Nature of Investors			
		Risk Averse	*Risk Neutral*	*Risk Taker*	*Total*
Investor Category	Fund Managers	1(11.1)(1)	4(44.4)(3.6)	4(44.4)(4.5)	9(100)(3)
	HNIs	1(4.2)(1)	15(62.5)(13.4)	8(33.3)(9.1)	24(100)(8)
	Retail Investors	79(36.6)(79)	76(35.2)(67.9)	61(28.2)(69.3)	216(100)(72)
	Intermediary Investors	19(37.3)(19)	17(33.3)(15.2)	15(29.4)(17)	51(100)(17)
Total		100(33.3)(100)	112(37.3)(100)	88(29.3)(100)	300(100)(100)

Source: Question No. 10 and 7 of the Questionnaire

Table 31
Chi Square Test

	Value	*df*	*Asymp. Sig. (2-sided)*
Pearson Chi-Square	13.973(a)	6	.030
Likelihood Ratio	17.341	6	.008
Linear-by-Linear Association	3.987	1	.046
N of Valid Cases	300		

Source: Output of SPSS

The significance value, from the Table 31, is found to be less than .05, Hence concluded that there is a significant relationship between the two variables, Nature of investors and the Investor category they belong to.

Conclusion

The above correlation and Chi-square analysis shows that there exists relationship between the personal factors and the Types of investors based on their risk-taking capacity and hence the null hypothesis is refuted.

The findings from the chis-square and cross-relationship analysis are summed up as follows:

- Age and Nature of investors are related.
- Education level of investors and nature of investors are associated.

- Occupational status of investors are highly associated with the natuer of investors.
- Experience in the field of investments correlate to the types of investors.
- There exists high correlation between the nature of investors and their tenure of investment, value of investments made and the related investor category.

5

Heuristic Behavioral Factors of Investors

The Investment Decisions are based on *market sentiments*[1]. In Behavioral Finance, "sentiment" is synonymous with "error". Several studies have identified influence of psychological factors on stock market. Daniel Kahneman (2000), reports that market has a psychology or a character. It has thoughts, beliefs, moods, and sometimes stormy emotions. The main characteristic of the market is extreme nervousness[2]. The market sways with the moods and powerful emotional preferences of investors.

Figure 1 discloses the investor's emotional cycle*. The mood of an investor changes from Exuberance to Complacency and Panic in the Emotional Life cycle. This is also reflected in market sentiments. The upheaval of Enthusiasm and Over Confidence due to recurring gains may decline drastically on a huge loss, causing repeated biasness in consecutive decisions. This Emotional cycle repeats again after a short span, on recuperation of the market.

It is full of hope one moment and full of anxiety the other day. The market may seem to be disturbed by the economic news such as inflation, global prices, change in government policies, RBI interest rates, and other related commercial news. The market at one point of time lifts the share value of a particular sector of economy and another day it may become hostile with that sector completely pulling it down, displaying an 'irrational exuberance' behavior. This volatile behavior of excessive optimism may push the stocks abnormally high, relative to its fundamental values. One of the predominant reasons for this stock market behavior is the reflection of the cognitive biases of Individual investors with different states of mind driving their decisions in capital market investments. Thus the fundamental errors of investors may cumulatively manifest in the security prices, and what is known as 'market sentiment'.

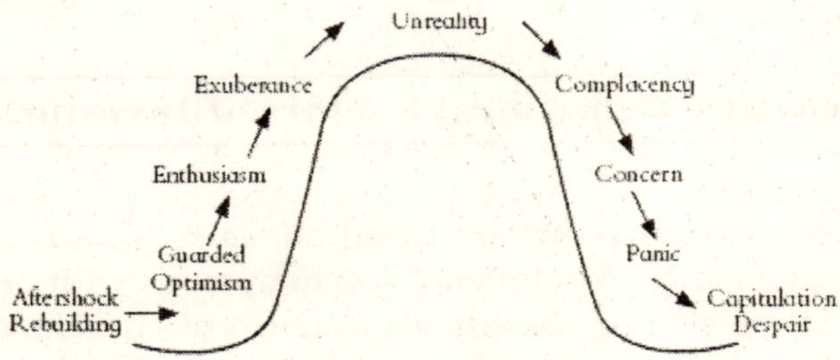

Where are we now?

Figure 1: The Investor's Emotional Lifecycle

Individuals often tend to use cognitive heuristics (or mental shortcuts) due to the difficulties experienced in assigning probability to the outcomes that are uncertain. There are errors that may occur in the exhibition of heuristic behavior of investors that may be described as decision bias.

Kahneman and Tversky[3] have explained the influence of investors' emotions in the decision-making process and what fallacies lead to judgmental errors resulting in financial loss or wrong decisions, as it is found that investors place different weights on gains and losses. They are willing to remain in a risky stock position by holding on the losing stock anticipating the prices to bounce back because they are more distressed by prospective losses than they are happy by equivalent gains.

In the light of the above discussion, this chapter attempts to identify the major heuristic behavioral factors that influences the Investors' decisions.

Statements Explaining the Heuristic Biases

Statements describing the heuristic variables in decisions are given in Part C, Question Number 1 to 49 (refer Appendix A).

These statements are self-explanatory in nature and these statements are used to identify the heuristic behavioral factors of investors and they were presented in a five point Likert scale ranging from Strongly agree to Strongly Disagree. The opinion of the respondents are reported in Table 1.

It is observed from Table 1, that 37.7 percent of the investors have strongly agreed with the variable "continue to hold securities personally selected". In respect of the variable "desire to take risk, to earn more returns", 39.7% of the respondents have expressed their opinion of agreement. Count on the variable "seeking advice from competent professionals", it is reported that 37.7 percent of the respondents have disagreed to this statement. Towards the variable "having expert knowledge and vast experience to play safe", it is found that 45.7% have agreement. 50.3 percent have agreed "avoiding error of judgment is impossible". The statement relating to "diligence in quickly responding to signals", 53% of the investors have strongly agreed. 52.7% of them agreed that "they have learnt a lesson on their past mistakes".

In respect of the variable "more weightage given to one's own views and opinion", 43.3% of the investors have agreed. Fifty percent of the respondents have disagreed with the statement "disregarding risk that doesn't support one's views" and 38.7% have disagreed with "ignoring to obtain complete information". Around 60% of the investors have agreed that "they prefer to invest in Bear market when the value declines". Majority of the respondents (72.3%) have agreed with "investment expecting possible returns".

A count on the statement "choice is based on superior information", it is found a disagreement of 37.3% of the investors. More than half of the investors have agreed that the "market will bounce back". "The optimism on future prospects after a successful gain", has an agreement from 45.7% of the investors. It has been found that 56.7% of them have agreed upon " investments were pursued on high possible returns".

Half the respondents found to have disagreed that "they are risk seekers". Around 50% of them have agreed that "they were confident in their own skills and judgment". It is reported

Table 1
Statements Explaining the Heuristic Behavior

Behavioral Statements	*SA*	*A*	*NO*	*DA*	*SDA*	*Total*
I continue to hold securities, I have personally selected	113(37.7)	93(31.0)	7(2.3)	84(28.0)	3(1.0)	300(100)
I love taking risk, to earn more returns	56(18.7)	119(39.7)	7(2.3)	81(27.0)	37(12.3)	300(100)
I always seek the advice of competent professional investors for selecting my investment	41(13.7)	105(35.0)	4(1.3)	113(37.7)	37(12.3)	300(100)
I have expert knowledge and vast experience in the stock market, that enables me to play safe always.	45(15.0)	137(45.7)	3(1.0)	109(36.3)	6(2.0)	300(100)
One cannot avoid the error of judgment.	133(44.3)	151(50.3)	10(3.3)	5(1.7)	1(0.3)	300(100)
One should be diligent to respond to misleading signals quickly.	159(53.0)	123(41.0)	1(0.3)	13(4.3)	4(1. 3)	300(100)
Several instances had made me learn from my past mistakes	116(38.7)	158(52.7)	6(2.0)	16(5.3)	4(1.3)	300(100)
I give more weightage for my views and opinions than the information I get while making my investment decisions.	118(39.3)	130(43.3)	1(0.3)	46(15.3)	5(1.7)	300(100)
I disregard risks that does not support my view	32(10.7)	111(37.0)	3(1.0)	150(50.0)	4(1.3)	300(100)
I tend to invest on my intuitive knowledge, ignoring to obtain complete information	60(20.0)	110(36.7)	2(0.7)	116(38.7)	12(4.0)	300(100)
I Invest in 'Bear' markets when my overall portfolio value declines	31(10.3)	181(60.3)	2(0.7)	79(26.3)	7(2.3)	300(100)
My investment is based on possible returns, even if they are uncertain	44(14.7)	217(72.3)	3(1.0)	34(11.3)	2(0.7)	300(100)
My choice is based on superior information; I need not know what information is available with the counter- party to trade	56(18.7)	75(25.0)	14(4.7)	112(37.3)	43(14.3)	300(100)
In a downturn share market, I believe that the market will bounce back	103(34.3)	153(51.0)	3(1.0)	34(11.3)	7(2.3)	300(100)
I am overly optimistic regarding future prospects followed by a successful investment experience	60(20.0)	137(45.7)	5(1.7)	89(29.7)	9(3.0)	300(100)
I pursue investments of high possible returns but low expected returns	67(22.3)	170(56.7)	8(2.7)	42(14.0)	13(4.3)	300(100)
I am a compulsive risk-seeker; I accept almost any degree of risk.	34(11.3)	75(25.0)	0(0)	151(50.3)	40(13.3)	300(100)
I am confident in my own skills and judgment in investing as distinct from others in the market, which proved successful in all my decisions	46(15.3)	157(52.3)	4(10.3)	81(27.0)	12(4.0)	300(100)
My intuition gives me strength and confidence to face the illusions and post judgment errors.	21(7.0)	195(65.0)	4(1.3)	74(24.7)	6(2.0)	300(100)
I will choose one of the investments with lower risk, when their expected returns are equal.	64(21.3)	219(73.)	0(0)	4(1.3)	13(4.3)	300(100)
While risk taking for greater losses, or a sure loss, I would seek the chance to recover my money rather than getting profits.	67(22.3)	207(69.0)	0(0)	21(7.0)	5(1.7)	300(100)

Contd.

Behavioral Statements	*SA*	*A*	*NO*	*DA*	*SDA*	*Total*
I am not confident on the information I have obtained nor do I have the ability to process it.	47(15.7)	80(26.7)	3(1.0)	110(36.7)	60(20.0)	300(100)
The speed with which information is disseminated and investors' ability to mobilize funds, cause price trends	116(38.7)	151(50.3)	3 (1.0)	17(5.7)	13(4.3)	300(100)
I read the documents accompanying an offer very carefully before my investment decision	70(23.3)	203(67.7)	4(1.3)	22(7.3)	1(0.3)	300(100)
I always make a complete and deep analysis of my potentials and available information before investing my funds.	99(33.0)	131(43.7)	2(0.7)	62(20.7)	6(2.0)	300(100)
Investors are not as diversified as they should be.	60(20.0)	182(60.7)	6(2.0)	49(16.3)	3(1.0)	300(100)
Investors have a lower propensity or intention to sell those stocks on which they have a capital loss	79(26.3)	146(48.7)	0(0)	70(23.3)	5(1.7)	300(100)
I am over confident about the future because of my ability to easily predict events	68(22.7)	91(30.3)	0(0)	122(40.7)	19(6.3)	300(100)
The investor knows that he is in a 'bubble'; it is advisable to stay in the market until it bursts	61(20.3)	130(43.3)	0(0)	80(26.7)	29(9.7)	300(100)
As a following agent, I choose the actions of the leading agents disregarding my own private information	51(17.0)	135(45.0)	5(1.7)	64(21.3)	45(15.0)	300(100)
I normally follow the crowd sentiment, due to convenience.	80(26.7)	104(34.7)	0(0)	80(30.0)	26(8.7)	300(100)
The group behavior implicates excess price volatility and affects the normalcy of the financial system.	113(37.7)	178(59.3)	0(0)	8(2.7)	1(0.3)	300(100)
Circuit breakers impose a trading halt in the face of substantial selling pressure to check the difference in interpretation, seems to be beneficial to the investors.	99(33.0)	168(56.0)	0(0)	26(8.7)	7(2.3)	300(100)
Experience and expertise in investments would lead to, more realistic and prompt investment.	141(47.0)	122(40.7)	4(1.3)	31(10.3)	2(0.7)	300(100)
Investors tend to over-react to negative information more zealously than to positive information.	128(42.7)	122(40.7)	3(1.0)	22(7.3)	25(8.3)	300(100)
Investors tends to follow the group, due to lack of confidence.	114(38.0)	129(43.0)	0(0)	50(16.7)	7(2.3)	300(100)
Investors trade on 'noise' (actions of others) as if it were information	94(31.3)	162(54.0)	1 (0.3)	26(8.7)	17(5.7)	300(100)
Investors in some instances neglect their private information in order to trade against the market.	107(35.7)	127(42.3)	2(0.7)	42(14.0)	22(7.3)	300(100)
On any price changes or dividend announcements, the markets over-react or under-react	112(37.3)	181(60.3)	0(0)	6(2.0)	1(0.3)	300(100)
Volatility of IPO is due to lack of fixation of a mindset regarding the company.	97(32.3)	160(53.3)	4(1.3)	36(12.0)	3(1.0)	300(100)
A company recorded 20% earnings growth last quarter and expects a smaller growth rate this quarter. But if the company records a 40% growth rate in earnings, we may brush aside the growth rate as temporary.	129(43.0)	127(42.3)	0(0)	40(13.3)	4(1.3)	300(100)

Contd.

Behavioral Statements	*SA*	*A*	*NO*	*DA*	*SDA*	*Total*
Under-reaction enables smart managers a chance to buy the stock cheap, before market realizes the under-reaction	160(53.3)	130(43.3)	0(0)	5(1.7)	5(1.7)	300(100)
The heterogeneity in information processing capability is the main reason of the price and volume patterns observed in the market	79(26.3)	197(65.7)	0(0)	16(5.3)	8(2.7)	300(100)
Large investors are generally better informed than small investors	69(23.0)	200(66.7)	0(0)	27(9.0)	4(1.3)	300(100)
Investors will have a disposition to hold on to losing stocks and sell winners	46(15.3)	223(74.3)	0(0)	19(6.3)	12(4.0)	300(100)
Selling of loosing stocks than the winners is done on the month of December	10(3.3)	137(45.7)	9(0.3)	123(41.0)	21(7.0)	300(100)
Investors seek to buy 'hot 'stocks and try to avoid stocks which have performed poorly in the recent past	108(36.0)	147(49.0)	4(1.3)	28(9.3)	13(4.3)	300(100)
Investors assume that recent events will continue in the near future	119(39.7)	153(51.0)	0(0)	16(5.3)	12(4.0)	300(100)
I Frequently check the market values to confirm if I had picked the right stock / stocks	112(37.3)	151(50.3)	5(1.7)	32(10.7)	0(0)	300(100)

Source: Part B -Question Nos. 1 to 49 of the Questionnaire

that 65% of them agreed that "their intuitions have given them strength to face illusions". 73% of the investors agree for a "choice on low risk and high return investment". It is observed that 69 percent of the respondents agreed that "on a sure loss, they prefer recovery of money invested than making profits". For the variable "less confidence on the information received and inability to process it", 36.7% have disagreed with this statement.

Fifty percent of the investors found to agree "that the speed dissemination of information and mobilizing funds for investment cause price trends". Majority of them (67.7%) have an agreement on the statement "thorough understanding on information of an offer made before investment decision taken". It is found that 43.7% have agreed that "they make deep analysis on information as also their potentials". Around 60% of them have agreed that the "investors are not as diversified as they should be".

Nearly 50% of the investors have shown their agreement on "low propensity to sell the stocks that have a capital loss". 40.7% have disagreed with the variable on "their over confidence in predicting the future events". 43.3 have agreed that "they are aware of the bubble, hence staying in market until it bursts is advisable". 45% have agreed that they "follow the decisions of leading agents".

It has been observed from the data that 34.7% of the investors tend to " follow the crowd". 59.3% have stated that they agree on "normalcy of financial system is affected due to crowd behavior". Majority of them (56%) agree that "circuit breakers are beneficial". Half the respondents agree that "experience and expertise would fetch better exposure for wise investments". 42.7% of the investors strongly agreed that "over-reaction for negative information is more vigorous than on positive information".

The data shows that 43% agree that "investors follow the crowd due to lack of confidence". More than 50% of them agree that "investors react rigorously on the actions of others". Around 42% of them have shown their agreement on "neglect of private information happens to beat the market". Majority of them (60%) agree that "people tend to over or under react for price changes and corporate announcements". 53.3% have agreed on "lack of knowledge on company leads to price variation in case of IPOs".

The data reveals the agreeableness and strongly agreeing level, as 42.3% and 43% on the statement pertaining to anchor on historical information by ignoring the current information. It is found that 53.3% of them to strongly agree on the variable that "smart managers react quickly to buy stocks at a cheaper price in downturn market".

It is agreed by 65.7% of the investors that the heterogeneity in processing information causes the price and volume patterns". In respect to the variable "large investors are better informed than retail investors", it is found that 66.7% have commonly agreed on this statement. An overall response of 74% are more clustered and convictional for the variable "investors tend to hold on losing stocks and sell winners". Also 49% have agreed that " preference for hot stocks is more than the poor performance stocks". Majority (51%) have agreed that "recent events will continue in near future" and finally 50 percent of them have agreed that "they often check the market values of the stocks picked by them".

The above percentage analysis on the data describe the emotional attitude of the investors in a general way. To gain a deeper understanding and to list out the dominant factors of heuristic behavior, the researcher has applied the Factor analysis for the data collected and they are processed through the SPSS package.

Justification for Application of Factor Analysis for the Data

The responses of the sample respondents on 49 variables selected to measure the heuristic behavior of investors has been stated in Table 1 in terms of frequency and percentage. Correlation matrix of variables leading to identification of heuristic behavioral factors are given in Table 4 in order to establish the relevance of application of Factor Analysis for the variables selected for this study, Barlett statistical test of

Sphericity was applied to the correlation matrix to measure and to quantify the degree of inter correlations among the variables and to the appropriateness of factor analysis. The result of the Barlett's test is reported in Table No. 2.

Table 2
KMO Bartlett's Test

Kaiser-Meyer-Olkin Measure of Sampling Adequacy.		.683
Bartlett's Test of SphericityApprox.	Chi-Square	12278.562
	df	1176
	Sig.	.000

Table No. 2, reveals that the probability test of Measure of Sampling Adequacy (MSA) for the selected variables is 0.683, which is above the threshold probability value of 0.50. The test result establishes that it has the significance value of less than .000 (where alpha value is 0.05). Since the variables selected for the study falls within the acceptable level, MSA supports our decision to perform the factor analysis on the sample data for the simple reason that the relationship between the set of variables selected in this study and the samples chosen for the study have established its significance through the Barlett's statistical test.

Analysis and Discussion on Heuristic Behavioral Factors

In order to identify the potent heuristic behavioral factors that influence the investor's power of decisions in stock market, Varimax Principal Component Factor analysis was applied to reduce the data relating to the 49 variables used in this study and for extracting the highly influential variables that compound and constitute the factors relevant for analysis.

Application of Varimax and Kaiser Normalisation Rotation on the sample data disclosed the factor loadings for each of the variables and reported in Table 3.

Table 3 shows the correlation matrix for the 49 variables on the investor's behavior, taken up for analysis to identify the factors. As has been stated earlier, the above correlations matrix was subject to Barlett's test (refer Table No. 2).

Table 3
Correlation Matrix of Variables on Heuristic Behavior

Statements	Variables												
	F1	F2	F3	F4	F5	F6	F7	F8	F9	F10	F11	F12	F13
S36	.797*	.142	-.039	.151	.234	.096	-.024	-.012	-.021	.198	.008	.145	.081
S37	.783*	-.048	-.053	-.234	.069	.033	.060	.376	-.019	-.050	.114	-.105	.137
S13	-.693*	.071	-.353	.057	.139	.078	-.173	-.041	-.112	.215	.140	.044	.018
S29	.654*	.211	.035	-.021	.005	-.018	.284	.282	-.137	.266	-.099	-.101	-.147
S35	.616*	.131	.269	.393	.316	.043	-.156	-.015	-.021	-.319	-.021	.088	.089
S38	.599*	.253	-.300	.126	.235	-.136	-.087	.001	-.108	.297	-.162	.028	.230
S32	.497	-.043	.065	.284	.153	.119	.278	.050	-.101	.248	-.176	.192	.318
S19	.229	.755*	.192	.010	.240	-.124	-.024	-.092	-.139	-.005	.071	-.039	.088
S28	.373	.697*	-.209	.003	-.153	-.251	.076	.042	-.121	.277	-.068	-.077	.026
S17	.022	.663*	.066	.240	.011	-.003	-.334	-.249	.003	.089	.038	.143	-.151
S2	-.117	.657*	.345	-.219	-.342	.156	-.268	.003	.004	-.057	-.139	-.007	.072
S18	.114	.506*	.089	.309	.063	.452	-.255	-.187	-.191	.036	.343	-.026	.134
S4	-.178	.476	.038	.152	-.042	.364	.024	-.231	.059	.398	-.032	-.271	.277
S3	-.467	-.472	.268	-.166	.290	.026	-.150	.308	.120	-.287	.016	.098	-.050
S15	-.203	.469	-.252	.065	-.256	.252	-.165	.108	-.217	-.026	-.264	.272	.292
S26	.005	-.014	.830*	.039	.077	.072	.100	-.151	-.035	.149	.063	.194	.031
S27	.066	.044	.819*	.059	-.045	.096	.110	.240	.021	-.030	-.031	-.179	-.048
S25	.041	.462	.626*	-.009	-.150	-.050	.103	.129	-.289	-.074	-.067	-.014	.078
S24	-.034	.129	.541*	.369	-.194	-.049	.241	.021	.216	-.147	.429	-.086	.132
S6	.186	.068	.039	.783*	-.025	-.095	.002	.103	.267	.177	.008	-.012	.037
S16	-.032	-.002	.044	.669*	.331	.280	.100	.280	-.006	-.128	-.208	.116	.115
S11	-.241	.062	.006	.584*	.139	.127	-.251	-.141	-.279	.162	.101	-.167	.341
S22	-.244	-.053	-.379	-.510*	.367	.245	-.015	-.014	.144	-.152	-.163	.209	-.149
S8	.312	.341	.301	.450	-.138	.366	.060	.133	-.034	.193	.249	.047	-.111

Contd.

Statements	Variables												
	F1	*F2*	*F3*	*F4*	*F5*	*F6*	*F7*	*F8*	*F9*	*F10*	*F11*	*F12*	*F13*
S7	-.090	.020	.026	.429	-.338	.209	-.367	-.296	.104	.018	.236	-.043	-.185
S31	.172	-.025	-.120	.080	.859*	-.031	.156	-.073	-.010	.067	-.008	.154	.092
S30	.147	-.085	.030	-.014	.836*	-.216	.208	.025	.149	.067	.069	.076	-.085
S44	-.032	-.003	.035	.025	-.084	.837*	-.036	.033	.065	-.017	.017	.162	-.258
S45	.071	-.123	.092	.023	-.146	.822*	.066	.171	.075	.072	-.045	-.158	.128
S46	-.143	.157	-.157	.347	-.096	.422	.275	-.196	-.139	.178	-.310	.038	.097
S42	.148	-.058	.152	-.101	.208	-.048	.828*	-.097	.051	-.002	.011	-.002	.046
S41	.086	-.091	.152	.141	.234	.137	.690*	.039	.035	.151	.002	.204	.175
S40	.050	-.127	.082	-.056	-.043	.106	.564*	.372	-.025	-.200	-.076	.265	.091
S9	.054	.385	-.043	-.042	.109	.266	-.541*	-.216	.146	.394	.108	-.055	.229
S12	.220	-.061	.307	.288	-.049	.092	.062	.724*	-.015	-.104	.234	-.069	.029
S14	.040	-.113	-.064	.415	.000	.291	.048	.690*	-.161	-.035	.039	-.169	-.064
S21	.124	-.118	-.031	-.148	-.062	-.086	.046	.674*	.104	-.024	-.234	-.072	.070
S34	.369	.024	.117	.004	.105	.432	-.008	.462	-.396	-.084	-.221	-.086	.224
S48	-.116	-.037	.018	.044	.032	.058	.052	.030	.892*	.155	-.065	-.027	-.082
S49	.024	-.204	-.155	-.014	.028	.014	-.032	-.041	.778*	-.157	.249	.122	.105
S47	-.034	-.077	.442	.234	.319	.078	-.098	-.058	.564*	-.331	-.273	.109	.029
S5	.193	.110	.070	.150	.087	.093	-.064	-.132	-.002	.805*	-.174	.062	.069
S1	-.200	-.072	.071	-.013	-.031	-.044	-.079	-.087	.062	-.148	**.829***	.192	.028
S10	.016	.279	-.222	.024	.335	-.078	-.053	-.068	-.016	.493	**.543***	.099	-.207
S43	-.022	-.006	-.031	.069	.206	.132	.256	-.102	.069	.040	.225	**.748***	.051
S39	.202	-.090	-.090	-.255	.085	-.281	.232	-.228	.243	.087	.171	**.551***	.028
S20	-.109	.226	.305	-.118	.391	-.224	-.062	-.191	-.082	-.014	-.330	.480	-.017
S33	.316	.152	.027	.128	.021	-.080	.199	.093	.022	.031	-.019	.048	**.661***
S23	.040	-.063	.223	.192	-.330	-.337	.264	.156	-.011	.408	.161	.150	.442

[* indicates correlations significant at the .01 level.
Overall Measure of sampling adequacy 0.683 with threshold value 0.50
Barlett's test of spherecity : 12278.562 . Significance .000]

Examination of the value for each variable and the resultant reduction of variables effectively meets the threshold of sampling adequacy with MSA value of .683.

Application of Varimax with Kaiser Normalization method to select number of components to be retained for further analysis is reported in Table No. 4.

Table No. 4 contains information regarding the thirteen possible factors and their relative explanatory power as expressed by their eigen values. All the total 13 factors extracted have got 1 as eigen value and account for a total variance of 78.728 (threshold value 60 %) . Out of the 13 factors, only 8 factors were retained and considered for analysis, which represent 64.88% of the variance explained through inter correlation between the variables of this study. The remaining 5 factors have not been considered for this study because of the insignificant inter relationship among these variables constituting these factors which are of minor importance for this study. Hence they are non-explanatory factors and undefined for the purpose of this study.

Finally, the most effective eight factors have been considered in this study through which this study has attempted to explain the heuristic behavior, commonly found on Investors in Stock Market, and these 8 heuristic factors are defined and named as follows;

1. Information Bias
2. Over-Confidence Bias
3. Discharge Effect Bias
4. Mindset Bias
5. Spill-Over Enthusiasm Bias
6. Situational Reaction Bias
7. Peripheral and Pre-Judged Bias
8. Gambler's Fallacy

Information Bias on Investor's Behavior

Information Bias refers to how people use familiar events and information to assess the probability of a future outcome. Rather than thoroughly researching a topic and weighing the

Table 4
Factor Matrix of Heuristic Behavior Variables

Factors	*Initial Eigen Values*			*Extraction Sums of Squared Factor Loadings*		
	Total	*% of Variance*	*Cumulative %*	*Total*	*% of Variance*	*Cumulative %*
E.F. – 1	7.041	14.370	14.370	7.041	14.370	14.370
E.F. – 2	5.702	11.636	26.006	5.702	11.636	26.006
E.F. – 3	4.688	9.567	35.574	4.688	9.567	35.574
E.F. – 4	3.827	7.810	43.383	3.827	7.810	43.383
E.F. – 5	3.297	6.729	50.112	3.297	6.729	50.112
E.F. – 6	2.706	5.523	55.635	2.706	5.523	55.635
E.F. – 7	2.453	5.006	60.641	2.453	5.006	60.641
E.F. – 8	2.082	4.249	64.889	2.082	4.249	64.889
Undefined	1.907	3.892	68.781	1.907	3.892	68.781
Undefined	1.441	2.940	71.721	1.441	2.940	71.721
Undefined	1.302	2.658	74.379	1.302	2.658	74.379
Undefined	1.128	2.301	76.680	1.128	2.301	76.680
Undefined	1.004	2.048	78.728	1.004	2.048	78.728

[Extraction Method: Principal Component Analysis.
Rotation Method : Varimax with Kaiser Normalization
E.F. – Explanatory Factor]

information objectively, people turn to the most accessible and convenient sources for guidance. This bias was identified through the following variable and they go together to explain the factor "Information Bias" that influence the Investors in decision-making and the statistical results are given in Table No. 5.

This may be one of the reasons why investment companies spend millions on advertising the track records of a few high-performing mutual funds within their entire fund family. They are betting that many consumers will choose funds according to name recognition or assume that perceived success in one specific fund infers equivalent skill in other fund categories.

This study found that the information bias is one of the dominant factors with factor loading of 7.041. This factor accounts for explaining the Information Biasness in Investor's Investment decision to the extent of 14.37% as against the total of 78.728%.

Discussion: Information Bias cause investors to over-react to market conditions whether it be "positive" or "negative". In the late 1990's, investors got caught up in tech mania, which caused them to disregard the risks. This was followed more recently by recession and market turbulence in the economy, which caused investors to lose confidence due to negative results on their investments. Information bias also causes people to think that events that receive heavy media attention are more important and pertinent than they are in actuality. Unfortunately, much of the financial information received on a daily basis is mostly noise and not particularly important. In fact, the information is often inaccurate, based on multiple opinions, outdated or downright confusing. Coupled with too much information, many investors overlook the fact that they often lack the training, experience and objectivity to interpret the massive amount of information available. This causes many investors to get a false sense of security in thinking they are well-informed investors.

Focusing on long-term results and to avoid getting swept away by the emotions and the latest mania whether it be positive or negative, it is required to recognize that most recent

Table 5
Factor 1-Information Bias

Variables	Eigen Value Factor Loading Values	Total	% of Variance	Cum. %	Total	% of Variance	Cum.%
Neglect of private information beat the market.	0.797						
Trade on 'noise'as if it were information	0.783						
Choice is based on superior information, information available with the counter- party not known	0.693						
In a 'bubble' it is advisable to stay in the market until it bursts	0.654	7.041	14.370	14.370	7.041	14.370	14.370
Tendency to over-react to negative information more zealously than to positive information.	0.616						
Follow the group, due to lack of confidence.	0.599						

Source: Q. No. 36,37,13,29,35,38 of Questionnaire

financial events proliferated by the news media are over-emphasized and not to be overly influenced by it. The old axiom, "nothing is as good or as bad as it seems" is important for the investor to keep in mind.

This bias could be eliminated by following accurate research that is presented scientifically and in context by objective sources, as well as certain professional and scholarly journals or rely on the fundamentals of the company.

Over Confidence Bias in Investor's Behavior

Over Confidence bias pertains to the pervasive tendency of people to think that they know more than they do, over-rating their own abilities, on subsequent gains in the market (Kahneman & Riepe, 1998)[4]. They also over-estimate the precision of their knowledge, relative to others. Over-Confidence and Irrationality are adaptive psychological traits that help one to survive in this world. Earlier studies have also reported that people are over-confident in their judgments (Barberis and Thaler, 2003)[5]. Over-Confidence again is an effect of irrational exuberance which results in excessive trades, with its trading costs denting profits.

This bias was explained through the variables that go together to explain the factor "Over Confidence Bias".The variables and the factor loadings of the heuristic factor 'over confidence bias' is reported in Table No. 6.

Over Confidence is the next prominent factor with factor loading of 5.702 (Table 6). This factor has emerged as second important factor in explaining the Investor's Bias in Investment decision to the extent of 11.636% as against the total of 78.728%. This factor alongwith the factor 'Information Bias' explain 26.006% of the total variance.

It is reported by the investors of the study that they are intuitively strong enough to face illusions and post judgmental errors with confidence. Investors over estimate their degree of control to predict the future events in the market. Confidence to take greater risk for earning more returns are running high with respect to sample respondents. All these reportings provide a detailed discussion for this factor as follows;

Table 6
Factor 2–Over Confidence

Variables	Values	Eigen Value			Factor Loading		
		Total	% of Variance	Cum. %	Total	% of Variance	Cum. %
Investors intuition gives strength and confidence to face the illusions and post judgment errors.	.755						
Investors are over confident about the future because of their ability to easily predict events.	.697						
Investors are compulsive risk-seeker and accept almost any degree of risk.	.663	5.702	11.636	26.006	5.702	11.636	26.006
Investors love taking risk, to earn more returns.	.657						
Investors are confident in their own skills and judgment in investing as distinct from others in the market, which proved successful in all their decisions.	.506						

Source: Q. No. 19,28,17,2,18 of Questionnaire

Discussion: Human behavior has instinctive behavioral patterns, stored in the brain for millions of years which are responsible for the daily routines such as getting up in the morning, taking coffee, having breakfast etc. These are programmed activities that often do not change at all during the course of a lifetime. These daily repeated life time chores are referred as 'Gut Feeling'(Jon Elster, 1999)[6]. This routine behavior when disturbed becomes problematic. For Investors in Financial markets the gut people are programmed for profits. Gut people are instinctive and generally take Intuitive decisions. In an environment that requires intensive trading within a short time frame (ie., in day trading) when they are unable to analyse the situations, the gut person will subsequently resort to heuristics ie., to simplify facts to make snap decisions. This type of investors are of material in nature and justify their actions when they run a loss. They are convinced of their own capabilities of making quick profits from favorable situations and this leads to Over-Confidence. This instinctive nature will make the gut persons to decide quickly, invest quickly and realize their profits quickly. They rarely panic on any uncontrollable situations or on incurring exorbitant losses, tend to be cool and normally cling on to their decisions very firmly. This intuitiveness and gut-feeling has triggered their level of confidence at a higher level.

Over Confidence bias may cause investors to overestimate their degree of control, resulting in more borrowing, making payments late with penalty etc. They are aggressive buyers and sellers. When a subsequent news confirms their judgment providing gains, they are overconfident in their ability more than justified but, when news refutes their judgment, their confidence level is less than warranted.

People who have specialized knowledge in market sectors, industries or professions may believe that their skills enhance their stock picking ability, especially in those areas of knowledge. This view typically begets overconfidence, which encourages excessive trading activity in an account. There are research studies to show that excessive trading incurs higher costs and larger doses of risk while driving down net returns below the market average and below the average returns earned by less active investors.

Experience is the most potent remedy for overconfidence. But it also inflicts pain and sacrifice of investor's wealth. The wiser investor has to understand the difference between speculating and investing—and avoid the get-rich-quick trading mentality. This over-confidence in the behavior of Investors normally observed from the respondents, arise out of their intuitions which has been successful in many instances, especially in an uptrend market, and the same has failed to be a correct judgment during a downtrend market.

Establishing an investment policy statement, and sticking on to it even at times when market surges ahead and thereby increasing confidence level, would help avoid wrong decisions. Psychologists have found that people become overconfident when they experience success. Even a novice investor experienced profits investing in technology stocks during the Tech bubble in 1990s, attributing much of their success to their ability to make wise investment decisions and this overconfidence has lead to financial losses on other stocks.

Discharge Effect Bias in Investor's Behavior

This bias has been identified through the variables, that go together to explain the factor "Discharge Effect Bias" that influence the Investors in decision-making. The results are reported in Table 7.

Discharge Effect Bias is the third important factor with factor loading of 4.688 (Table 7). This factor has emerged as the third important factor in explaining the Investors' Bias in Investment decision to the extent of 9.567% as against the total of 78.728%. All the three factors viz., Information Bias, over confidence bias and the discharge effect bias account for 35.574% of the total variance reported.

Discussion: To avoid the loss of regret on investing in loss-making stocks. Investors generally follow the tendency of Selling winners and keeping losing stocks, which is termed as the Discharge effect Bias. As such, this behavior might be perfectly compatible with complete rationality as it seems to

Table 7
Factor 3–Discharge Effect Bias

Variables	*Values*	*Eigen Value*			*Factor Loading*		
		Total	*% of Variance*	*Cum. %*	*Total*	*% of Variance*	*Cum. %*
Investors are not as diversified as they should be.	.830						
Investors have a lower propensity or intention to sell those stocks on which they have a capital loss.	.819						
Investors always make a complete and deep analysis of their potentials and available information before investing in funds.	.626	4.688	9.567	35.574	4.688	9.567	35.574
Investors will have a disposition to hold on to losing stocks and sell winners	.541						

Source: Q.No. 26,27,25,24 of Questionnaire

be. This is more applicable to those day-traders who don't take positions on their trades. The disposition effect is the observation that investors show a more aggressive contrarian behavior according to which investors are prone to hold winners too long and sell losers too early to make immediate gains.

Under Discharge effect, investors are risk averse when faced with gains and risk-seeking when faced with losses. It seems that the investors frame their choices in terms of potential gains and losses, and, they behave as if evaluating the decision consequences on an S-shaped value function, which is concave for gains and convex for losses. This behaviour reflects risk aversion in the gain region and risk-seeking in the loss region.

It could also be around that the discharge effect moves the investor to his risk averse or risk - seeking part of the value function so that he intends to reduce or increase his position in the risky assets; the final result being he sells winners and holds losers.

In view of the discharge effect people dislike incurring losses much more than they enjoy making gains. People are willing to gamble in the domain of losses, to catch up what they have lost so far.

Henceforth, holding stocks that have lost its value and with an urge to sell stocks that have risen but before it reaches its peak value. Discharge Effect bias can be avoided by setting long-term goals for the portfolio. The decision of selling winning stocks or holding losing stocks has to be decided based on the stock's fundamentals.

Mindset Bias in Investor's Behavior

The investors' mindset is 'fixed and keep' holding stocks based on the market value and their investment behavior is adjusted through the mental accounting according to the current market situation coupled with the external opinion. This Mindset bias appears to influence on heuristic behavior. The data given in Table No. 8 explain the Mindset Bias and the dependence of investors on mental accounting and framing bias.

Mindset bias is another important factor identified to understand the heuristic behavior of investors, which has a factor loading of 3.827 (Table No. 48). This factor has emerged as fourth important factor in this study to explain the Investor Biasness in Investment decision to the extent of 7.810% as against the total of 78.728%. This factor along with the first three factors explained earlier account for a total variance of 43.38%.

Discussion: The investors tend to exhibit 'heuristics', applied for immediate decisions. Certain critical situations may need to resolve the decision problem as quickly as possible. Heuristics are used to arrive at a quick judgement as required by the circumstances, especially in day trading. When estimating probabilities, individuals "anchor" or "fix their mind" on a specific value and then adjust it to account for other elements of the circumstance. Usually once the anchor is set, there is a bias toward that value.

For instance, even the most prudent investors may anchor their overall return expectations to the sensex and Nifty indexes. When the market drastically deviates from the particular average, investors begin to question whether the nature of markets has changed. After a prolonged period of abnormal returns, some investors begin adjusting their long-term views to match recent experience, despite the fact that even a prolonged period of variance is not unusual. This illustrates recency bias, which is the opposite of mindset bias. People can give too much weight to recent experience and extrapolate recent trends that are at odds with long-term averages.

The remedy to mindset and recency bias is to adapt a statistical view of the long term and to use the most appropriate benchmarks when assessing performance or comparing specific investments. In financial markets, particularly on a volatile market, in case of day trading, the current situation usually serves as an anchor, if there is no additional information available regarding the company or economy. External information collected for instance, from the analysts is also considered as an anchor. Mindset Bias is typified as a

Table 8
Factor 4 - Mindset Bias

Variables	*Values*	*Eigen Value*			*Factor Loading*		
		Total	*% of Variance*	*Cum. %*	*Total*	*% of Variance*	*Cum. %*
One should be diligent to respond to misleading signals quickly.	.783						
Investors pursue investments of high possible returns but low expected returns	.669						
Investors Invest in 'Bear' markets when their overall portfolio value declines.	.584	3.827	7.810	43.383	3.827	7.810	43.383
Investors are not confident on the information they have obtained nor do they have the ability to process it.	.510						

Source: Q. No. 6,16,11,22 of Questionnaire

phenomenon, that is inherent in the process of estimation[7]. It need not necessarily be a numerical value, such as the spot prices of stocks. It can also be based on the opinions or attitudes of experts or friends. The opinion or an information pronounced by the expert or an analyst would be anchored in the minds of the investors, which reflects in the trading activity on that day. This anchoring effect on decisions might be successful at times. For instance, the fall in crude prices on 18th, July 2008, followed by the experts' opinion about a few sectors, impacted on the reversal of the market trend, from a low of 12500 sensex index to 13866, a surge of 1300 points, on 21st July, 2008. But unwitting investors don't grasp the severity of their risk until potential losses become real losses which is too late to realise.

Mindset Bias also has the effect of 'Frame Dependence' or 'Mental Accounting'. Mental Accounting, is a common process adopted by any human being. It is the different ways of arranging and keeping accounts in mind, to enable oneself decide in the best possible manner. It is also referred as the "hedonic framing". This refers to people's tendency to partition their finances into categories. One example of mental accounting is when a retiree separates his portfolio into "safe" and "risky" categories, with the "safe" investments designed for principal protection and the "aggressive" investments intended for growth. The approach often results in higher risk from over-concentration in a single stock, sector or asset group— and higher expenses and taxes due to inefficient portfolio management.

In financial markets the investors gains and losses are evaluated and weighed as different mental accounts, to deduce finally that their decisions are not bad, when compared with others. For instance, if an investor has produced a very bad or negative returns on his investment, over a period of time, he would integrate with the successful period in the past and conclude that their overall position is not very bad. If a person has gained Rs.20000 on a portfolio and lost Rs. 10000 on another, he would contend himself that he earned a profit of Rs. 10000. But ultimately the pleasure of gains earned is comparatively lesser than the displeasure on his losses incurred. All these mental calculations fixes the mind of investors towards irrational behaviour.

Spill-Over Enthusiasm Bias

Investors more openly acknowledge the impact of emotion on their investment decisions. Spill Over Enthusiasm is a mentality characterized by a lack of individuality, causing people to think and act like the general population. This factor is used in the investing world to describe the forces that cause unsubstantiated rallies on sudden sell-offs and buying of stocks.

The variables and their values accounting for creation of this factor is given in Table 9. Spill-Over Enthusiasm is another important factor with a factor loading of 3.297 (Table 9). This factor has emerged as an important factor in explaining the Investor Biasness in Investment decision to the extent of 6.729% as against the total of 78.728% and the 50.112% total variance is explained along with the other factors discussed earlier.

Discussion: Investors tend to conform to the behavior of the majority or 'mass psychology'. Investors often blindly follow the group, presuming that the group is always right. Such group of investors are concerned with short term gains and thus have very short-term planning horizons. Investors in the capital market are generally prone to spell-over enthusiasm or 'following the crowd', a situation where the buyers are willing to overpay on their stock picks than the actual fundamental values. Due to this decision bias, investors tend to chase returns rather than accomplishing their goals.

Spill-Over enthusiasm is a mental short-cut method, developed because it is a cost-effective way of learning, from the experience of successful people, to earn profits easily and at a much faster scale. The new entrants normally the risk-averse group of investors in the market, adopt this behaviour who lack experience, as a measure to avoid taking risk.

It appears from the market crashes and bubbles, that this behavior of Spill-Over Enthusiasm, both optimistic and pessimistic is one of the primary reason for excess price

Table 9
Factor 5 – Spill- Over Enthusiasm

Variables	*Values*	*Eigen Value*			*Factor Loading*		
		Total	*% of Variance*	*Cum. %*	*Total*	*% of Variance*	*Cum. %*
Investors normally follow the crowd sentiment, due to convenience.	.859						
As a following agent, Investors choose the actions of the leading agents disregarding their own private information	.836	3.297	6.729	50.112	3.297	6.729	50.112
The group behavior of Investors implicates excess price volatility and affects the normalcy of the financial system.	.822						

Source: Q. 31,30,32 of Questionnaire

volatility and fragility of the financial system. When a crisis situation demands a crucial decision requiring immediate response, investors tend to disregard their own private information and follow the crowd, as a safe guarding measure. Investors are more prone to mental shortcuts, like any sudden drop in the market is a good time to buy instead of analyzing its fundamentals, or any news shared about a specific stock in a meeting or a get together, there is the chance, of its value reflected in the market. It is found that, more the degree of risk aversion, there is a strong impulse to do what others are doing or to blindly follow the market.

Situational Reaction Bias

Individuals overestimate their own abilities in various contexts. The situational reaction bias can be either over or under reacting to the current news, positive/negative which is reflected in the sudden increase or decrease of the stock prices far away from their fundamentals.

The stock market 'overreaction' hypothesis asserts that stock prices take temporary swings away from their fundamental values due to waves of optimism and pessimism. Investors' reactions to stock market volatility is examined through some of the variables and the result of the analysis are shown in Table 10.

It is observed from the Table 10, that Situational Reaction Bias is the sixth important factor with a factor loading of 2.706 and explains the Over/ Under Reaction Bias on Investment decisions to the extent of 5.523% as against the total of 78.728%. Along with the other five factors, it accounts for 55.635% of variance.

Discussion: In financial markets, Analysts and Investors generate information for trading through various means, such as interviewing management, verifying rumors, analyzing financial statements, and execute them with varying degrees of skill. If an investor overestimates his ability to generate information, or to identify the significance of existing data that others neglect, he will underestimate his forecast errors. If he is more overconfident about signals or assessments with which

Table 10
Factor 6 – Situational Reaction Bias

Variables	*Values*	*Eigen Value*			*Factor Loading*		
		Total	*% of Variance*	*Cum. %*	*Total*	*% of Variance*	*Cum. %*
Under-reaction enables smart managers a chance to buy the stock cheap, before market realizes the under-reaction.	.828						
A company recorded 20% earnings growth last quarter and expects a smaller growth rate this quarter. But if the company records a 40% growth rate in earnings, investors may brush aside the growth rate as temporary.	.690	2.706	5.523	55.635	2.706	5.523	55.635
Volatility of IPO is due to lack of fixation of a mindset regarding the company.	.564						
Investors disregard risks that does not support my view	.541						

Source: Q.No. 41,40,9,42 of Questionnaire

he has greater personal involvement, he will tend to be overconfident about the information he has generated but not about public signals. Thus, an overconfident investor will overestimate with precision the private information signal, and not the information signals publicly received by all.

Stock prices tend to overreact to private information signals and underreact to public signals[16]. For example, a rationally managed firm may tend to buy back more of its stock when managers believe their stock is undervalued by the market. In such cases, the corporate event will reflect the managers' belief about the market valuation error, and will therefore predict future abnormal returns.

Many instances of over and under reaction of investor's behavior in market can be attributed to positive news of a company For example– Announcement of post earnings And stock split have resulted in Over-reaction leading to increase in the stock prices. Similarly some positive corporate announcements like Acquisition or Bonus Issue have also shown under-reaction resulting in decline of its stock prices. The jitters caused in the minds of investors that the price paid to acquire the stocks has been overly estimated and unreasonable. This behavioral bias of over reaction with an intention of booking huge profits had proved to be fatal, in case of IPOs resulting in tremendous losses to the investors in the event of listing of these shares. This experience seems to have affected further IPOs, due to under reaction and henceforth withdrawal of IPOs by the companies.

This situational reaction , both over and under reaction causes the extreme panic or exuberance in the stock market, and avoidance of such hyper reaction might keep the volatility in control.

Peripheral and Pre-judged decision Bias

Efficient markets, risk management, asset class diversification are some of the key areas in financial planning that drives the investors to make rational choices with their money. While rational behavior appears to rule in the entire stock markets, it often falters at the individual level. It seems that, many investors act on impulse, emotion and illusion and are forced to pay a high price for their mistakes. When investors act on impulse, they fall prey to market myths, false hopes and financial illusions.

The Peripheral and Pre-judged biases are investors illusions and beliefs about the recent events happened in the stock market presuming to have expected to happen. These cognitive biases affect the rational decisions of investors. In Peripheral bias, importance is given to the recent events rather than the fundamental values of the stocks.

The Peripheral and Pre-judged bias is the seventh important factor with a factor loading of 2.453. This factor has emerged as an important factor to explain the Investor Biasness in Investment decision to the extent of 5.006% as against the total of 78.728%. Alongwith other factors, this factor accounts for a total variance of 60.641 as given in Table No. 11.

Peripheral or Recency Bias is one of the cognitive biases, which affects the rational decision making of investors It happens, when a person assigns greater value to the most recent piece of information observed. For Example : *If a driver sees an equal total number of black cars and red cars during a long journey, but there happens to be a glut of black cars at the end of the journey, he or she is likely to conclude that there were more black cars than red cars throughout the drive. Similarly, sports fans assume that a few excellent performances are proof of a player's underlying ability. So, would be investors, who may assume that a mutual fund's record over the past year is a reliable indicator of the manager's skill*[8].

Pre-Judged bias is the ability of the investors to think and visualize the actual events before they occur. Investors' find it easy to draw conclusions now about past market cycles, sector performance, the economy's direction, or about winning/losing stocks. Pre-Judged bias induce investors to believe that the signs are obvious all along, but in reality, that the signs are obvious only in retrospect.

It appears that, many individual and institutional investors rely on past experience to predict the future. Their rules-of-thumb rarely pay off, however, investors learn from their past mistakes, since investments in stock market deals with the

Table 11

Factor 7– Peripheral and Pre-judged decision Bias

Variables	*Values*	*Eigen Value*			*Factor Loading*		
		Total	*% of Variance*	*Cum. %*	*Total*	*% of Variance*	*Cum. %*
Investment is based on possible returns, even if they are uncertain.	.724						
In a downturn share market, Investors believe that the market will bounce back.	.690	2.453	5.006	60.641	2.453	5.006	60.641
While risk taking for greater losses, or definite loss, Investors would seek the chance to recover their money rather than getting profits.	.674						

Source: Q.No.12,14,21 of Questionnaire

unknowable future. The best approach to avoid this bias is to manage uncertainty by diversifying across many asset groups and markets, based on investor's ability to accept risk.

Gambler's Fallacy Bias

Gamblers' fallacy can be considered to be an extreme belief in regression to the mean. Regression to the mean is found in many human systems and implies that an extreme trend will tend to move closer to the mean over time. For example, an upward trend must be followed by a downward trend in order to satisfy a law of averages.

The variables explaining Gambler's Fallacy and the factor loading are reported in Table 12. Gambler's Fallacy is the last factor with a factor loading of 2.082 with a variance of 4.249% against the total variance of 78.728%. All the eight factors identified together explain a total of 64.889% variance.

Discussion: Gamblers' fallacy arises when people inappropriately predict that a trend will reverse. This tendency may lead investors to anticipate the end of a run of good (or poor) market returns. Investors in the financial markets also fall victim to the gambler's fallacy, as they act on the belief, " What comes down , must go up", which to some extent has been true. After a downfall of the market, majority of the investors expected rising index and hold on to their stocks longer than on an average.

It has been a false assumption that most market crashes takes place in October. The Indian Market experienced heavy losses on July 2008 which was one of the biggest fall shedding around 9000 points from 21206 points to 13111 mark, over a period of six months from 10th January 2008 tumbling down to 8695 points as on November 25, 2008. The bullish phase from September 2001, when the sensex was 2595, was a tenfold increase upto Jan 2008.

The turbulence in the market in 2008 or in many instances in the past, are associated with numerous factors but the information and the news were exacerbated by the psychological sentiments and emotions of the investors to a great extent, which had a major impact on the Stock Market

Table 12
Factor 8 – Gambler's Fallacy Bias

Variables	*Values*	*Eigen Value*			*Factor Loading*		
		Total	*% of Variance*	*Cum. %*	*Total*	*% of Variance*	*Cum. %*
Investors assume that recent events will continue in the near future.	.892						
One cannot avoid the error of judgment.	.778						
Investors seek to buy 'hot 'stocks and try to avoid stocks which have performed poorly in the recent past.	.564	2.082	4.249	64.889	2.082	4.249	64.889

Source: Q.No.48,49,47 of Questionnaire

Meltdown, and if it would have been avoided, the losses also wouldn't have been so huge.

Hence with the gambler (the trader that isn't following any formula or system (i.e not trading to the laws of probability) is not making any rational decisions. Individuals sometimes make rational decisions, and sometimes make intuitive decision. Sometimes intuition is better, sometimes rationality is better. They take intuitive decisions when they think they are making rational decisions. Or perhaps more brazenly, intuition will hijack cognition bias.

Conclusion

This chapter identified heuristic behavioral factors that impel investors to make irrational investment decisions based on the biases implicit in each of the factors. These heuristic factors or bias in decisions are:

1. Information Bias
2. Over-Confidence Bias
3. Discharge Effect Bias
4. Mindset Bias
5. Spill - Over Enthusiasm Bias
6. Situational Reaction Bias
7. Peripheral and Pre-Judged Bias
8. Gambler's Fallacy

However, there are some of other minor factors, which may have little significance in decisions but the above eight factors are found to be having profound influence in irrational investment decisions of Indian Investors based on sentiments, emotions and cognitive biases as explained in the above eight heuristic factors.

The predominant eight factors have been put to further analysis to find out if they have any influence on the types of investors and also on their average returns earned from the investments in stock market which is discussed in the other chapters of the study that follows.

Footnotes

1. Hersh Shefrin, (2005), "A Behavioral Approach to Asset Pricing", *Academic press Advanced Finance series*, pp 203-204.
2. *Ibid.*, 205-206.

* Source: The DeVoe Report, "What's a Bull Market, Dad?"

** Source: Tony Brabazon (2000), "Behavioral Fianance: A new sunrise of a false dawn".

3. Daniel Kahneman and Amos Tverksy, (1979), "Prospect Theory: An Analysis of Decision Under Risk," *Econometrica*, Vol. 47 pp 263-291.
4. Kahneman, D. and Riepe, M.W. (1998). "Aspects of investor Psychology", *Journal of Portfolio Management*, Vol.24, Iss.4, pp.52-65.
5. Nicholas Barberis, Ming Huang and Richard Thaler, (2006),"Individual Preferences, Monetary Gambles, and Stock Market Participation: A Case for Narrow Framing"), *American Economic Review* 96, pp.169-175.
6. Jon Elster, (1999), Alchemies of the mind: Rationality and the emotions, Cambridge University Press, pp. 285-287.
7. Mary Kynn, "The 'heuristics and biases' bias in expert elicitation", (2007), Journal of the Royal Statistical Society: Series A (Statistics in Society), Volume 171, Issue 1 , pp 239-264.
8. Hogarth, Robin M, Einhorn, Hillel J., (1992), 'Order Effects in Belief Updating: Belief-Adjustment Model', *Journal of Cognitive Psychology*, Vol. 24 Issue 1, pp 15 - 18.

6

Personal Factors, Investment Profile and Return on Investments

Investing is the process of giving up something now in order to receive something in future. Taking risk in investments is giving up something known now without knowing what your return will be in future. The Loss Aversion is inherent in our self, which means losses hurt more than gains provide us pleasure. People react emotionally to money and their reactions affect their financial success.

Profiling and typographies help individuals to become better investors by highlighting deficiencies in investment style and behavior or how an investor is interacting with the market-for example, trading too frequently selling too early, inability to cut losses, or a failure to use information effectively[1].

Association between Personal, Investment Factors and Earned Return

Return earned on Investment is generated by a financial decision taken for investing in an asset class or selecting a diversified portfolio wherein each asset provides an income over a period of time. Earned Return unlike earned income which has the obvious advantage, that it's the only type of income that doesn't require an upfront investment (other than time) to make money, shall reap benefits only on investing on the right assets. The downside is that the amount of Earned Income you can make is limited by the amount of time you are willing/able to invest and once you stop working, you stop making money but in case of Earned Return, the density might vary according to choosing of the right assets, like real estate, gold, mutual funds etc.

The Average Earned Return is generally influenced by some of the Personal and Investment factors of the Investors. The significance of relationship between these factors have been assessed using ANOVA. The dependent variable has been taken as Average Earned Return and associated with the Independent variables such as, Age of respondents, Educational qualification, Occupational category, Experience, Tenure of Investment, Investor category, Value of Investment, Basic nature of Investors, Expected rate of Return, and Basis of decision. The data relating to above association are presented in Table No. 1 to 23 and taken up for discussion in the following paragraphs.

Analysis and Discssion

The following Null hypothesis have been developed to examine the relationship of the personal and investment factors with their Returns earned on their investments.

H_3: The personal factors do not have any significant relationship with the Earned Returns of the Investors.

H_4: There does not exist any significant relationship between investment profile of investors with their Earned returns on investment.

Association between Average Earned Return and the Age of the Respondents

The data relating to the variable Average Return Earned and the age of the respondents are shown in Table No. 1.

In normal situations, the earned return increases with the age factor, but in case of Investment in capital market, it depends on the decisions taken by the investors, irrespective of the age of the respondents. It is inferred from the data in Table No. 1, that 42.9 percent of the respondents within the age group of 30 to 40 years have reported to have earned a return between 30 and 40 years. 27.5% of the respondents in the age group of 40 and 50 years are earning returns on an average above 50 percent. 41.8% of the respondents in the age group of 20 to 30 years are reported to have earned returns between 30 and 40 percent. More than 50 percent of the respondents in the age group above 40 years earned a return greater than 40 percent . Those who were in the age group of 20 and 30 years, one - fourth were earning less than 20 percent and the remaining three - fourth have shown a good return of above 30 percent.

At an early age above 20 years to 30 years, some of them who are in their initial stages of career, the requirement of funds is high, but have lesser investible funds. Hence they take lesser risk due to, either lack of experience and exposure in the stock market or due to lack of surplus funds for investment purposes due to which their returns found to be moderate. But, some of the young investors, employed in the well paid IT sector, especially in Bangalore, with surplus disposable income have entered the stock market taking a moderate risk, have gained better leverage over the other investors of above 40 years of age.

The investors in the age group of 30 and 40 years, who are in the prime of earning adequate income and also having the urge of churning higher returns from their surplus funds, the risk taking ability is quite high, having the opportunity for constructing a larger portfolio, consisting of high-yielding assets, have shown a good return of 30 percent and above. The investors between 20 to 30 years, with limited disposable/ surplus funds tend to be risk averse and cautious in deciding their portfolio, more concerned with safety of their investment and satisfied with moderate returns.

Thus it can be concluded that majority in the age group of 20 and 30 years have earned satisfactory returns of 30 to 40 percent and those of 30 to 40 years have shown good returns on their investments and those above the age group of 50 years, have earned only moderate returns. These results are based on their respective risk taking ability also which is discussed in Chapter VII.

Table 1
Average Earned Return and Age of the Respondents

AER	*Age of the Respondents*				*Total*
	20- 30 Years	*30 - 40 Years*	*40 - 50 Years*	*50 and Above*	
> 40%	17 (32.1)(21.5)	2 (3.8)(7.1)	28 (52.8)(27.5)	6(11.3)(6.6)	53(100)(17.7)
30% to 40%	6(7.6)(7.6)	12(15.2)(42.9)	30(38)(29.4)	31(39.2)(34.1)	79(100)(26.3)
20% to 30%	33 (33.3)(41.8)	0 (0.0)(0)	32(32.3)(31.4)	34(34.3)(37.4)	99(100)(33)
10% to 20%	6(17.6)(7.6)	9(26.5)(32.1)	7(20.6)(6.9)	12(35.3)(13.2)	34(100)(11.3)
10% to -10%	17(48.6)(21.5)	5(14.3)(17.9)	5(14.3)(4.9)	8(22.9)(8.8)	35(100)(11.7)
Total	79(26.3)(100)	28(9.3)(100)	102(34)(100)	91(30.3)(100)	300(100)(100)

Source: Primary data Question No. 1 and 13

Table 2
Average Earned Return and Age of Respondents

Age of the Respondents	*Mean*	*N*	*Std. Deviation*
20- 30 Years	3.00	79	1.377
30 - 40 Years	3.11	28	1.343
40 - 50 Years	2.32	102	1.101
50 and Above	2.84	91	1.036
Total	2.73	300	1.217

The above explanation is also supported by the results given in Table 2. The mean value (3.11) is the highest among the age group of 30 and 40 years with a standard deviation of 1.343 and the mean Average Earned Return is lowest among the respondents in the age group of 40 to 50 years with a SD of 1.101.

Application of F test for the above data relating to Age of the respondents and Average Earned Return are shown in Table No. 3.

From Table No 3, it could be inferred that the F Value (6.554) shows a significant result as it is less than .01. Hence it may be concluded that the Average Earned Return is different among the different age group accepting that the age of the respondents has significant relationship with their Average Earned Return and disapproving the null hypothesis.

Association between Average Earned Return and the Level of Education of the Respondents

The data relating to the variable Average Return and the Education level of the respondents are shown in Table No. 4.

Educational qualifications normally hold a higher value integrated with any profession or career. The study needs to understand whether the level of Education is associated with the Investments in Stock market. The data in Table No.4, reveals that higher returns of above 40 percent was found among the Post Graduates and Professionals than the other lesser qualified respondents.

Those with lesser qualification, majority of the graduates have earned a moderate return of 20 to 30 percent. Among

Table 3
ANOVA

		Sum of Squares	*df*	*Mean Square*	*F*	*Sig.*
Average Earned Return and Age of the Respondents	Between Groups	27.600	3	9.200	6.554	.000
	Within Groups	415.530	296	1.404		
Total		443.130	299			

Table 4

Average Earned Return and Educational Qualification of the Respondents

AER	*Educational Qualification of the Respondents*					
	Sec.	*H.Sec.*	*Grad.*	*P.Grad.*	*Professionals*	*Total*
> 40%	15(28.3)(71.4)	2(3.8)(10.5)	8(15.1)(10.5)	1(1.9)(1)	27(50.9)(33.8)	53(100)(17.7)
30% to 40%	0(0)(0)	0(0)(0)	3(3.8)(3.9)	55(69.6)(52.9)	21(26.6)(26.3)	79(100)(26.3)
20% to 30%	3(3)(14.3)	14(14.1)(73.7)	43(43.4)(56.6)	23(23.2)(22.1)	16(16.2)(20)	99(100)(33)
10% to 20%	2(5.9)(9.5)	1(2.9)(5.3)	11(32.4)(14.5)	9(26.5)(8.7)	11(32.4)(13.8)	34(100)(11.3)
10% to -10%	1(2.9)(4.8)	2(5.7)(10.5)	11(31.4)(14.5)	16(45.7)(15.4)	5(14.3)(6.3)	35(100)(11.7)
Total	21(7)(100)	19(6.3)(100)	76(25.3)(100)	104(34.7)(100)	80(26.7)(100)	300(100)(100)

those 20 to 30 years of age 28 percent have earned a return above 40 percent Thus it can be concluded that the higher the level of education, higher the returns. In other words, education contributes to a greater extent in increasing the returns on the investment in stock market, according to the data collected. But there are other factors like Experience in the investment field, Type of investor etc., which influences the Return on Investment.

Table 5
Average Earned Return and Educational Qualification of the Respondents

Educational Qualification of the Respondents	*Mean*	*N*	*Std. Deviation*
Secondary	1.76	21	1.300
H. Secondary	2.33	19	1.251
Graduate	2.85	76	1.121
Post graduate	3.05	104	1.080
Professional	3.18	80	0.970
Total	2.73	300	1.217

The results are supported from the mean values obtained as shown in Table No.5. The mean value (3.18) is the highest for the group of investors who are Professionals with a standard deviation of 0.970 and the mean Average Earned Return is lowest among the respondents who are less educated (ie.,1.76) with a SD of 1.300.

The significance value from the Table No.6 is found to be less than .01, hence the given model is considered to be statistically significant at 1 percent level among the variables Education and Earned Return.

Association between Average Earned Return and the Experience of the Respondents

The data relating to the variable Average Return and the Experience of the respondents are shown in Table 7.

It is believed that experience in any job or profession adds more wisdom and knowledge in the field whoever is associated with. More the experience in any job also enhances

Table 6
ANOVA

		Sum of Squares	df	Mean Square	F	Sig.
Average Earned Returns and Educational Qualification	Between Groups	51.864	4	12.966	9.776	.000
	Within Groups	391.266	295	1.326		
	Total	443.130	299			

Table 7

Average Earned Return and Experience of the Respondents

AER	Experience of the Respondents				Total
	< 5 years	*5 to 10 years*	*10 to 15 years*	*> 15 years*	
> 40%	18(34)(16.2)	5(9.4)(7.7)	1(1.9)(1.8)	29(54.7)(43.3)	53(100)(17.7)
30% to 40%	7(8.9)(6.3)	23(29.1)(35.4)	28(35.4)(49.1)	21(26.6)(31.3)	79(100)(26.3)
20% to 30%	48(48.5)(43.2)	26(26.3)(40)	21(21.2)(36.8)	4(4.0)(6.0)	99(100)(33)
10% to 20%	14(41.2)(12.6)	5(14.7)(7.7)	5(14.7)(8.8)	10(29.4)(14.9)	34(100)(11.3)
10% to -10%	24(68.6)(21.6)	6(17.1)(9.2)	2(5.7)(3.5)	3(8.6)(4.5)	35(100)(11.7)
Total	111(37)(100)	65(21.7)(100)	57(19)(100)	67(22.3)(100)	300(100)(100)

their income. This may or may not happen in case of investments in stock market. To analyse this aspect the data in Table 7 reveals that majority of the respondents earned less than 20 percent who had lesser experience in the investment field ie., below 5 years, whereas more than 75 percent of them having more experience greater than 15 years have earned a higher return of more than 40 percent.

The data reveals that higher the experience in the field of Investment in Stock market, higher the returns earned.

The analysis of the data has revealed that greater experience in stock market investment yields higher returns. The mean value is higher for higher the experience in stock market (3.17) and lesser mean value for lower experience (2.06) as shown in Table 8.

Table 8
Average Earned Return With Experience

Experience of the Respondents	*Mean*	*N*	*Std. Deviation*
> 15 years	3.17	111	1.299
10 to 15 years	2.75	65	1.031
5 to 10 years	2.63	57	.816
< 5 years	2.06	67	1.229
Total	2.73	300	1.217

The Anova Table 9, shows the significance level at less than .01, hence it is deduced that the variables experience in Stock market and Earned Return is statistically significant.

Association between Average Earned Return and the Tenure of Investment of the Respondents

The data relating to the variable Average Return and the tenure of investment of the respondents are shown in Table No. 10.

A key step in investment planning is defining the time horizon, or the length of time to work on the investment goals. In a highly volatile market experienced from January 2008 onwards, many investors had been thinking of throwing in the towel and quitting equity funds altogether, as the losses were susceptible in the current downtrend market. Real-estate and investment in metals, gold and oil, were considered as a

Table 9
ANOVA

		Sum of Squares	*df* *Square*	*Mean*	*F*	*Sig.*
Average Earned Return* Experience of the Respondents	Between Groups	52.296	3	17.432	13.202	.000
	Within Groups	390.834	296	1.320		
	Total	443.130	299			

Table 10
Average Earned Return and Tenure of Investment

AER	Tenure of Investment				
	long Term	Intermediate	Short Term	Speculative	Total
> 40%	6(11.3)(14.6)	3(5.7)(27.3)	20(37.7)(10.6)	24(45.3)(40)	53(100)(17.7)
30% to 40%	8(10.1)(19.5)	1(1.3)(9.1)	58(73.4)(30.9)	12(15.2)(20)	79(100)(26.3)
20% to 30%	10(10.1)(24.4)	6(6.1)(54.5)	63(63.6)(33.5)	20(20.2)(33.3)	99(100)(33)
10% to 20%	7(20.6)(17.1)	1(2.9)(9.1)	23(67.6)(12.2)	3(8.8)(5)	34(100)(11.3)
10% to -10%	10(28.6)(24.4)	0(0)(0)	24(68.6)(12.8)	1(2.9)(1.7)	35(100)(11.7)
Total	41(13.7)(100)	11(3.7)(100)	188(62.7)(100)	60(20)(100)	300(100)(100)

long-term investment and not advised as a short-term speculative investment. Beating markets with a long-term investment horizon, is that silver lining in the predominant grey clouds, for an investor, to earn good returns over a period of 5 to 10 years. A risk-averse person can also choose an actively managed diversified fund with a five-year investment horizon and achieve index-beating returns in this bearish market.

Similarly Intermediate and short-term funds provides both medium returns and ensures liquidity of funds. From the data, in Table 69, an attempt was made to assess the Earned Returns in terms of the tenure of investment chosen by the respondents. Majority of the speculative investors earned a return more than 40 percent. Nearly one-third of the investments made for short-term period, has given a good return of 20 percent to 40 percent. Around one-third of the investors have earned a return less than 10 percent and for the remaining investors, has given a moderate gains ranging from 30 percent to 40 percent.

It can be concluded from the data, during the boom period of stock market, more number of speculative and short-term investments has reaped good gains for the investors than the intermediate and the long term investors.

Table 11
Average Earned Return vs. Tenure of Investment

Tenure of Investment	*Mean*	*N*	*Std. Deviation*
long term	3.17	41	1.395
intermediate	2.45	11	1.036
short term	2.86	188	1.163
speculative	2.08	60	1.046
Total	2.73	300	1.217

The data in Table 11 reveals has a higher mean value for long term investment (3.17) followed by short-term investments (2.86) . Hence it can be concluded that the returns are higher with respect to higher the tenure of investment.

The ANOVA analysis in Table 12, pertaining to the variables Earned Return with Tenure of investment, at 1 percent significance level, reveals a value less than .01 and

Table 12
ANOVA

		Sum of Squares	df	Mean Square	F	Sig.
Average Earned Return * Tenure of Investment	Between Groups	36.892	3	12.297	8.960	.000
	Within Groups	406.238	296	1.372		
	Total	443.130	299			

hence observed that the two variables are statistically significant.

Association between Average Earned Return and the Value of Investments made by the Respondents

The data relating to the variable Average Return and the value of investments made by the respondents are shown in Table 13.

The Average Earned Return is directly related to the value of investment or the Total Amount invested in capital market. The data reveals that the returns of majority of the investors' ie., around 94 percent of the respondents having an investment value of less than Rs. 5 lakh, is found to be less than 20 percent. More than 90 percent of the investors having a value of more than Rs.15 lakh have earned returns above 40 percent . And those with an investments between Rs.5 lakh and Rs. 10 lakh have earned a moderate gain of 20 to 30 percent. From the data, it can be concluded that higher investment has given higher returns and those with lesser amount of investment have earned minimum returns. Hence it can be deduced that more the investment value has fetched handful gains.

Table 14 has proved the results in Table 13, with the higher mean value (2.99) for greater the investment and lesser mean value (1.20) for less investment made in the stock market.

The ANOVA analysis in Table 15, pertaining to the variables Earned Return and Value of investment, at 1 percent significance level, reveals a value less than .01 and hence observed to be statistically significant.

Association between Average Earned Return and Expected Rate of Return of the Respondents

The data relating to the variable Average Return and Expected rate of return of the respondents are shown in Table 16.

An expected return in financial risk is an extra return, to overcome the fear of loss of money. An expected return is a projected return that already averages out mathematically the probabilities of gains and losses. The Expected Returns are

Table 13
Average Earned Return and Value of Investments

AER	Value of Investment				Total
	< Rs. 5 lakh	*Rs. 5 lakh to Rs.10 lakh*	*Rs.10 lakh to Rs. 15 lakh*	*> Rs.15 lakh*	
> 40%	23(43.4)(13.8)	4(7.5)(4.1)	3(5.7)(30)	23(43.4)(92)	53(100)(17.7)
30% to 40%	47(59.5)(28.1)	27(34.2)(27.6)	5(6.3)(50)	0(0)(0)	79(100)(26.3)
20% to 30%	39(39.4)(23.4)	59(59.6)(60.2)	0(0)(0)	1(1)(4)	99(100)(33)
10% to 20%	25(73.5)(15)	7(20.6)(7.1)	1(2.9)(10)	1(2.9)(4)	34(100)(11.3)
10% to -10%	33(94.3)(19.8)	1(2.9)(1)	1(2.9)(10)	0(0)(0)	35(100)(11.7)
Total	167(55.7)(100)	98(32.7)(100)	10(3.3)(100)	25(8.3)(100)	300(100)(100)

usually high when compared to the Actual Earned Returns. The Expectations on Returns while entering, especially in a capital market is very high, since the returns in other investment avenues are relatively known. The gains in a capital market for a new entrant is a hype and hence the expectation on short span huge profits, are also invariably high. From the Table 16, majority of the investors' expected returns are 40 to 50 percent. Out of 5 respondents who have expected only 20 percent returns, 4 respondents have declared that they have earned only 20 percent gains. More than 50 percent of the total respondents have expected returns more than 50 percent, which is a common behaviour of the investors' in capital market. Out of those who have expected more than 50 percent returns, 48 percent of them have gained 30 to 40 percent returns and only 19 percent of the them have gained more than 50 percent.

Table 14
Average Earned Return and Value of Investments

Current Value of Investment	*Mean*	*N*	*Std. Deviation*
> Rs.1500000	2.99	167	1.335
Rs.1000000 to Rs. 1500000	2.73	98	.697
Rs.500000 to Rs. 1000000	2.20	10	1.317
< Rs.500000	1.20	25	.707
Total	2.73	300	1.217

Though the Expected and Earned returns are inversely related, the Earned Returns are observed to be considerably satisfactcry from the above data analysis, and this seem to be reliable due to the upward movement of the market, during the research period.

The Average Earned Return is higher within the range of 30 percent to 50 percent as expected by majority of the investors during the study period, when the market was in the upward trend with the mean value of (3.33 and 3.29) but with a normal returns of less than 20 percent on an average (mean value 4.80).

Table 15
ANOVA

		Sum of Squares	df	Mean Square	F	Sig.
Average Earned Return* Current Value of Investment	Between Groups	72.452	3	24.151	19.285	.000
	Within Groups	370.678	296	1.252		
Total		443.130	299			

Table 16
Average Earned Return and Expected Rate of Return

AER	*Expected Rate of Return*					*Total*
	> 50%	*50% to 40%*	*40% to 30%*	*30% to 20%*	*< 20%*	
> 40%	33(62.3)(18.9)	2(3.8)(5)	3(5.7)(12.5)	15(28.3)(26.8)	0(0)(0)	53(100)(17.7)
30% to 40%	51(64.6)(29.1)	15(19)(37.5)	1(1.3)(4.2)	12(15.2)(21.4)	0(0)(0)	79(100)(26.3)
20% to 30%	85(85.9)(48.6)	3(3)(7.5)	8(8.1)(33.3)	3(3)(5.4)	0(0)(0)	99(100)(33)
10% to 20%	3(8.8)(1.7)	8(23.5)(20)	10(29.4)(41.7)	12(35.3)(21.4)	1(2.9)(20)	34(100)(11.3)
10% to -10%	3(8.6)(1.7)	12(34.3)(30)	2(5.7)(8.3)	14(40)(25)	4(11.4)(80)	35(100)(11.7)
Total	175(58.3)(100)	40(13.3)(100)	24(8)(100)	56(18.7)(100)	5(1.7)(100)	300(100)(100)

Table 17
Average Earned Return and Expected Rate of Return

Expected Rate of Return	*Mean*	*N*	*Std. Deviation*
> 50 %	2.38	175	.869
50% to 40%	3.33	40	1.385
40% to 30%	3.29	24	1.122
30% to 20%	2.96	56	1.595
< 20 %	4.80	5	.447
Total	2.73	300	1.217

The ANOVA analysis in Table 18, pertaining to the variables Earned Return and Expected Return, at 1 percent significance level, reveals a value less than .01 and hence observed to be statistically significant.

Association between Average Earned Return and Types of Investors

The data relating to the variable Average Return and types of investors are shown in Table 19.

Risk in normal terms, denotes the precise probability of specific eventualities. It is the degree of uncertainty associated with a return on an asset. The field of behavioral finance focuses on human risk-aversion, asymmetric regret, and other ways that human financial behavior varies from what analysts call "rational". Risk is proportional to both the expected losses which may be caused by an event and to the probability of the unexpected variability or volatility of returns that includes both potential 'worse-than-expected' as well as 'better-than-expected' returns. Recognizing and respecting the irrational influences on human decision making may do much, to reduce disasters caused by naive risk assessments that pretend to be rational but in fact merely infuse many shared biases together.

Risk aversion is the reluctance of a person to accept a bargain with an uncertain payoff rather than another bargain with a more certain, but possibly lower, expected payoff. Risk aversion is measured as the additional marginal reward an investor requires to accept the additional risk.

Table 18
ANOVA

		Sum of Squares	*df*	*Mean Square*	*F*	*Sig.*
Average Earned Return* Expected Rate of Return	Between Groups	67.320	4	16.830	13.211	.000
	Within Groups	375.810	295	1.274		
Total		443.130	299			

A risk-neutral measure is a probability measure that results when one assumes that the current value of all financial assets is equal to the expected value of the future payoff of the asset discounted at the risk-free rate whereas, Risk-Taker expects more than normal returns for which he is willing to accept any future loss.

Table 19
Average Earned Return with Types of Investors

Average Earned Return	*Basic Nature of Investors* Risk Averse	Risk Neutral	Risk Taker	*Total*
> 40%	*4(7.5)(4)*	*29(54.7)(25.9)*	*20(37.7)(22.7)*	*53(100)(17.7)*
30% to 40%	7(8.9)(7)	48(60.8)(42.9)	24(30.4)(27.3)	79(100)(26.3)
20% to 30%	59(59.6)(59)	15(15.2)(13.4)	25(25.3)(28.4)	99(100)(33)
10% to 20%	8(23.5)(8)	16(47.1)(14.3)	10(29.4)(11.4)	34(100)(11.3)
10% to -10%	22(62.9)(22)	4(11.4)(3.6)	9(25.7)(10.2)	35(100)(11.7)
Total	100(33.3)(100)	112(37.3)(100)	88(29.3)(100)	300(100)(100)

Around 59 percent of the Risk Averse investors have an Earned Return of 20 to 30 percent and only a minimum of 10 percent were able to earn more than 40 percent. In case of Risk Takers and Risk Neutral investors, it was found that above 50 percent of them were earning more than 30 percent. This trend is also related to the favourable market movement for the investors.

Table 20
Average Earned Return and Type of Investors

Basic Nature of Investors	*Mean*	*N*	*Std. Deviation*
Risk Takers	3.37	100	1.031
Risk Neutralists	2.27	112	1.107
Risk Avoiders	2.59	88	1.247
Total	2.73	300	1.217

The mean value of 3.37 is higher in case of Risk Takers whereas is lower in case of risk Avoiders with a mean value of 2.59 which approves the results obtained.

The ANOVA Table 21, shows a significant value of less than .01 and hence concluded that both variables Earned Return and Nature of investors has significant relationship.

Association between Average Earned Return and Investors' Category of the Respondents

The data relating to the variable Average Return and Investors Category of the respondents are shown in Table 22.

Fund Manager are the person(s) responsible for implementing a fund's investing strategy and managing its portfolio trading activities. The individuals involved in fund management (mutual, pension, trust funds or hedge funds), are the professionals whose efficiency matches with the performance of fund.

High Net worth Investor (HNI) is a person, having investible assets (financial assets not including primary residence) in excess of US$1 million. The number of high net worth individuals worldwide is estimated at 9.5 million. HNI wealth totals US$37.2 trillion, representing a 11.4% gain since 2005. Ultra High Net worth Investors have at least US$30 million in investable assets. The number of ultra high net worth individuals worldwide is estimated at about 95,000[(6)].

Retail Investors are the Individual investors referred as small investors who buy and sell securities for their personal account, and not for another company or organization, who buy in much smaller quantities than larger institutional investors.

Intermediary Investor or Institutional Investor is a non-bank person or organization that trades securities in large quantities or value that they qualify for preferential treatment and lower commissions. Institutional investors face fewer protective regulations because it is assumed that they are more knowledgeable and better able to protect themselves.

The Table 22 reveals, Three-fourth of the fund managers with good results earned above 40 percent returns. The HNIs, around 80 percent of them have agreed that they earned best returns above 30 percent. The Intermediary investors have earned a moderate returns of 20 to 30 percent. And 50 percent of the retail investors have consented that their returns were

Table 21
ANOVA

		Sum of Squares	*df*	*Mean Square*	*F*	*Sig.*
Average Earned Return * Basic Nature of Investors	Between Groups	66.583	2	33.291	26.259	.000
	Within Groups	376.547	297	1.268		
Total		443.130	299			

Table 22
Average Earned Return and Investors Category

AER	Investors Category				Total
	Fund Managers	HNIs	Retail Investors	Intermediary Investors	
> 40%	6(11.3)(66.7)	9(17)(37.5)	28(52.8)(13)	10(18.9)(19.6)	53(100)(17.7)
30% to 40%	0(0)(0)	11(13.9)(45.8)	59(74.7)(27.3)	9(11.4)(17.6)	79(100)(26.3)
20% to 30%	1(1)(11.1)	1(1)(4.2)	79(79.8)(36.6)	18(18.2)(35.3)	99(100)(33)
10% to 20%	0(0)(0)	3(8.8)(12.5)	24(70.6)(11.1)	7(20.6)(13.7)	34(100)(11.3)
10% to -10%	2(5.7)(22.2)	0(0)(0)	26(74.3)(12)	7(20)(13.7)	35(100)(11.7)
Total	9(3)(100)	24(8)(100)	216(72)(100)	51(17)(100)	300(100)(100)

moderate and another 25 percent agreed that their returns were less than 10 percent and sometimes incurred losses also.

The ANOVA Table 23, shows a significant value of less than .01 and hence concluded that both variables Earned Return and Investor Category has significant relationship.

Heuristic Behavioral Factors and Average Earned Returns

This part of the chapter examines the relationship between each of the behavioral biases (identified in the earlier chapter) and the average earned return. The results of the analysis is shown in Table 24.

In the Table 24, it is to be seen that the behavioral factors have a statistically significant relationship with the Average Earned Return except for Discharge effect Bias and ituational Reaction bias.

Investors' Preferences for Investments

An attempt is also made to study the investor's preferences for investment. Question 50 of the instrument used for data collection has been analysed using the rank correlation method based on the ranking provided by the investors prioritizing their preferences of their investments.

It is observed from the Table 25, that investors top priority to invest is in Aggressive Growth fund, as it gives additional gains from equity investments during the surge in market betting on a GDP of 9 percent during the 2006- 2007. The least preference is given to Long term convertible debentures due to lack of Liquidity and lesser returns not preferable when market is booming. This trend may change on varying market conditions. Growth and balanced funds were also considered preferable investment choice by the investors.

Conclusion

This chapter examined the existence of relationship between (a) Personal factors and average earned return and (b) Investment factors and average earned return. The F Test was used to examine the relationship and the null hypothesis developed are rejected. It is concluded that;

Table 23
ANOVA

		Sum of Squares	*df*	*Mean Square*	*F*	*Sig.*
Average Earned Return * Investment Category						
	Between Groups	21.704	3	7.235	5.082	.002
	Within Groups	421.426	296	1.424		
Total		443.130	299			

Table 24
Correlation of Behavioral Factors and Average Earned Return

Factors		*Average Earned Return*
Information Bias	Pearson Correlation	.138(*)
	Sig. (2-tailed)	.017
	N	300
Over Confidence	Pearson Correlation	.249(**)
	Sig. (2-tailed)	.000
	N	300
Discharge effect Bias	Pearson Correlation	.089
	Sig. (2-tailed)	.122
	N	300
Mindset Bias	Pearson Correlation	.214(**)
	Sig. (2-tailed)	.000
	N	300
Spill-Over Enthusiasm Bias	Pearson Correlation	.112
	Sig. (2-tailed)	.052
	N	300
Situational Reaction Bias	Pearson Correlation	.011
	Sig. (2-tailed)	.846
	N	300
Peripheral and Pre-Judged Bias	Pearson Correlation	.349(**)
	Sig. (2-tailed)	.000
	N	300
Gambler's Fallacy	Pearson Correlation	.329(**)
	Sig. (2-tailed)	.000
	N	300

* Correlation is significant at the 0.05 level (2-tailed).
** Correlation is significant at the 0.01 level (2-tailed).

Table 25
Rank Correlation

Ranks	*Rank I*	*Rank II*	*Rank III*	*Rank IV*	*Rank V*	*Rank VI*	*Rank VII*	*Rank VIII*	*Rank IX*	*Rank X*	*Weighted Score =Σ (cell value *weighted score)*	*Priority*
Weighted Score	10	9	8	7	6	5	4	3	2	1		
Aggressive Growth Fund	166	4	16	17	4	1	2	42	1	28	2136	1
International Stock Funds	19	19	118	43	7	1	29	34	2	2	1877	2
Emerging Growth Funds	11	6	38	120	26	7	5	39	14	3	1667	3
Balanced Funds	4	4	20	55	105	3	29	14	24	5	1477	4
Growth and Income Funds	1	32	18	3	5	128	31	16	11	15	1342	5
High Yield Bonds	1	31	25	11	38	30	55	39	19	13	1332	6
Money Market Funds	2	79	1	0	1	45	23	4	36	67	1213	7
Arbitrage Funds	31	64	0	1	1	2	1	1	41	114	1112	8
Short Term Convertible Debentures	31	7	9	2	40	36	9	71	52	3	1055	9
Long Term Convertible Debentures	2	18	24	14	37	9	82	5	61	8	1050	10

- Personal factors viz., age, education, experience, occupational status and types of investors have significant relationship with the average earned returns
- Investment factors viz., tenure of investment, value of investments, expected **rate** of return and investor category have significant relationship with the average earned returns.
- The heuristic behavioral factors have a statistically significant relationship with the average earned returns, except for discharge effect bias and situational reaction bias.
- Investors prefer to invest in aggressive growth fund and give least preference to long term convertibles.

In furtherance of the analysis, the following chapter attempts to study the existence of the impact of behavioral biases with the types of investors and the magnitude of risk taking ability in each type of investors.

Footnotes

1. Jonathan Myers, (1999), "Profits without Panic - Investment Psychology of Personal Wealth", Nicholas Brealey Publishing Ltd., pp. 169-180.

7

Types of Investors and Heuristic Biases

Investors have been classified into three categories for the purpose of this study. This study has also identified eight dominant heuristic behavioral factors. It is assumed that these heuristic behavioral factors have strong influence on the types of investors. These decision biases in each of the heuristic factor varies from investor to investor depending on what category the investor fall ie., Risk Avoiders, Risk Takers and Risk Neutralists. The levels of these decision biases based on each of the above eight factors may cumulatively and individually affect each of the type of investors. Hence, an attempt is made to examine the relationship between the type of investor and the heuristic bias in the following paragraphs. For the purpose of understanding the nature of relationship between these variables, F test was applied with Two-way analysis.

Investor Types

Psychologists have become increasingly involved in attempting to classify investors. Barnwell classifies investors as a two-way model[1], (i) Passive investors and (ii) Active investors.

Passive investors are characterized as individuals who have become wealthy passively - by inheriting, by a professional career, or by risking the money of others rather than their own money. To these investors, security of money is more important than risk, hence are more risk conscious and likely to follow the investment herd. *Active investors*, are those who have achieved significant wealth, or earned well, during their own lifetime. They are more likely to take risks in investing because they have previous experience of taking risks in their previous wealth creation. These individuals have a high-risk tolerance and less of a need for security.

Paul Krugman, detects the behavioral traits of investors as, 'the seven habits of highly defective investors'[2], namely;

- Think short-term
- Be Greedy
- Believe in the greater fool
- Run with the herd
- Over-generalize
- Be Trendy
- Play with other people's money

And identifies some of the characteristics of an irrational investor as;

Too self-confident	exaggerates their own skills and its importance
Too Bold	an 'optimistic bias', believing that their chances are better than others
Too Timid	makes bold forecasts but rather makes timid decisions, also risk-averse
Too afraid of loss	reluctant to admit that they were wrong, hence hold on losing stock

Another Authority has identified investors' profile as: The "I Can't Stop Worrying Investor", The Power Investor, The Inheritor, The Impulsive Investor, The Gambler, "The Make Me Safe Investor", and The Confident Investor[3] (John Schott, 1998).

Bailard, Biehl and Kaiser propounded a five-way model[4] in describing the types of investors. This model as depicted in the graphic representation (Figure 1), projects the level of confidence an investor has in any decisions taken which is reflected in the emotional choices, ranging from Confident to Anxious and careful to Impetuous. The 'Adventurers' are strong willed and ready to take risk; 'Celebrities' want to be in limelight in choosing the latest investment, but least idea about control of finances; 'Individualists' are highly confident, methodical, balanced and analytical 'Guardians' older in age, cautious, shunning excitement or volatility; ' Straight Arrows' not on any extreme, balanced and moderate approach taking moderate risk.

"Money attitudes influence our behavior, aspirations and emotional reactions to ourselves, our families and our friends. Understanding your money style will help you gain insight into how and why you react emotionally to money"- Kathleen Gurney (2005). The nine money personalities, stresses the money style and how individuals react emotionally to financial decisions[5].

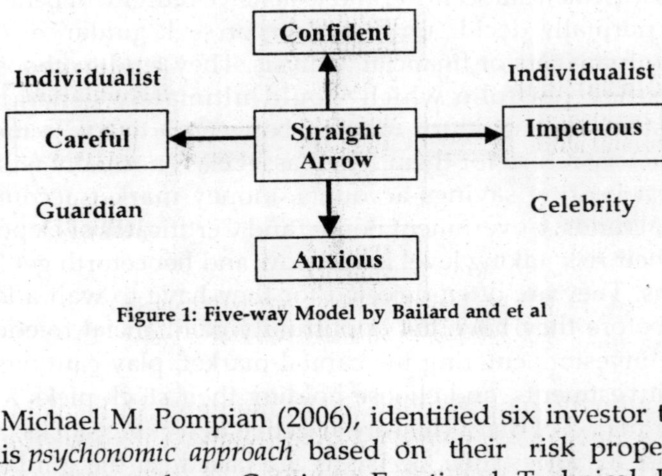

Figure 1: Five-way Model by Bailard and et al

Michael M. Pompian (2006), identified six investor types in his *psychonomic approach* based on their risk propensity and innate such as Cautious, Emotional, Technical, Busy, Casual and Informed[6].

These above classifications are mainly based on the heuristics or the judgment errors influencing the capital market investments. The application of psychology to financial behavior helps to avoid many of the investment pitfalls caused by human error. Hence this study endeavors, to associate the decision biases based on the degree of risk taken by the investors.

For the purpose of the study, the respondent investors have been classified into three categories on the basis of their ability to take risk in the market. There are also other criterion, such as, analytical skills and other attributes which also goes with risk-taking ability. The identification of investors into the above three categories are based on their own responses for the question Number 11 in the questionnaire (refer Appendix). Hence for further analysis in this chapter the characteristics of each category of investors have been described in detail in the following paragraphs.

Risk Avoiders

Investors who are risk averse, normally are very conservative. They seek low risk growth of capital and return, investing for long-term financial security, and to achieve retirement benefits. They normally decide on their own or seek guidance from money managers or financial analysts. They tend to choose a diversified portfolio which would ultimately generate a consistent annual return ranging between 3 to 8%, a much satisfactory return for them. Their asset class normally will be interest bearing savings accounts, money market accounts, Mutual funds, Government Bonds, and Certificates of Deposit, etc. Their risk taking level is very low and henceforth get low returns. They are often dejected for they have to wait a long time before they have the opportunity of financial freedom. These investors entering the capital market, play cautious in their investments, and choose holding their stock picks for a longer period of time. They are selective in picking stocks, and in most instances their decisions are based on the guidance from financial analysts. They become very dejected when their choice has gone wrong and affected at a great extent by investing in losing stocks.

Risk Takers

Risk Takers are normally the hard core Speculators, who choose to take control of their investments. They always look for an investing edge taking a chance of getting rich at a fast pace. Normally they tend to forego the relatively low returns of a portfolio in order to achieve a much higher returns on their Aggressive or 'hot' stock picks, and some may opt for investing from borrowed funds expecting a broad leap in returns. Their decisions are highly risky where if it proves correct the returns are huge and if it is biased, to earn little or no profits, ultimately leading to a large erosion of funds, after paying brokerage commissions, taxes and other investing fees. He is very much a gambler, who recognizes the potential gains more often from smart investing based on the experience gained in the stock market.

Risk Neutralists

The Savvy and Rational Investors fall under this category. They are moderate in taking decisions and most often tend to be risk neutral. They can be categorized as Specialists who have realized that there is a more powerful investing strategy than diversifying across a range of asset classes. They understand that the key to successful investing isn't luck or 'hot tips' but depend upon their education and experience. They generally pick a single investing area, and become experts in that area. They normally act on their plan, forward-looking, and adopt strategy by doing their homework to understand the risk side and where possible to reduce it. They are rational speculators who has understood the key tenets of serious investment success and intelligently predict from their intuitive knowledge. They are more analytical and fast in taking decisions.

Investor Type and Heuristic-Driven Biases

This study as already identified eight heuristic factors (refer chapter - IV) which drives the investors in decision-making. These biases are:

(1) Information Bias

(2) Over-Confidence Bias

(3) Discharge Effect Bias

(4) Mindset Bias

(5) Spill-Over Enthusiasm Bias

(6) Situational Reaction Bias

(7) Peripheral and Pre-Judged Bias

(8) Gambler's Fallacy Bias

Now attempt is made in the following paragraphs to analyse the relationship between the types of investors and the above dominant biases identified by this study .

Analysis and Discussion

The following Null hypothesis have been developed to examine the impact and magnitude of each heuristic biases affecting the Types of Investors .

H_5 : The types of investors are not influenced by any of the identified heuristic biases.

Types of Investors and Information Bias

The data relating to the different types of investors and the Information Bias as an instrument of heuristic factor is presented below in Table 1.

Table 1
Type of Investors and Information Bias

	Information Bias			
Type of Investor	*Low*	*Moderate*	*High*	*Total*
Risk Avoiders	69 (69.0)(89.6)	26(26.0)(25.7)	5(5.0)(4.1)	100(100)(33.3)
Risk Neutralists	0(0.0)0(0.0)	36(32.1)(35.6)	76(67.9)(62.3)	112(100)(37.3)
Risk Takers	8(9.1)(10.4)	39(44.3)(38.6)	41(46.6)(33.6)	88(100)(29.3)
Total	77(25.7)(100)	101(33.7)(100)	122(40.7)(100)	300(100)(100)

Heuristics bring *cognitive biases* in the decision making process. They on their turn cause market activity and price distortions. The data from Table 6, reveals that low level of Information Bias was more or less the same among the Risk Neutralists and Risk Takers. But moderate level of Information Bias was more among the Risk Takers than the Risk Avoiders. The high level of Information Bias was found among the Risk Neutralists.

The reason behind this is the Risk Neutralists found to be more analytical and this might cause 'Information biasness' in them. The Information Bias, consists of gathering so much information, whatever may be relevance and reliability that they get drowned in it and cannot find the leading thread to understand the issue. This might cause availability heuristics which is a cognitive bias or oversimplification of any fact, to arrive at immediate conclusion in times of emergency, which narrows the reasoning and decision-making. According to the Information bias, people tend to heavily weight their decisions toward more recent information, making any new opinion biased toward that latest news. In other words Information Bias contributes to a greater extent in the decision making process for Risk Neutralists. These findings concurred with those of Ellsberg[7] (1961), Thaler[8] (1994) and Barberis[9] (2001).

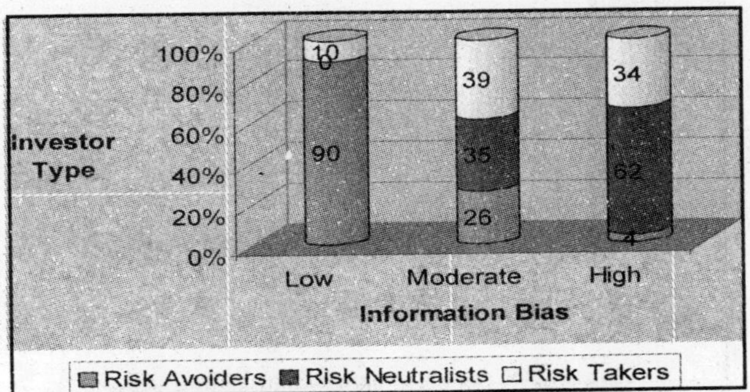

Figure 2: Information Bias and Type of Investor

From the ANOVA Table 2, it is understood that, F value is 30.07 and the Significance value is less than .01. Hence the above model is statistically significant at 1% level and hence found significant relationship between the variables Investor type and Information Bias.

Types of Investos and Over Confidence

It is found from Table 3 the data on level of Over Confidence is low for Risk Avoiders compared with others, and all three investor category have moderate level of Over-Confidence. High Level of Over Confidence is found among Risk Neutralists followed by the Risk Takers.

Table 2
ANOVA

		Sum of Squares	*df*	*Mean Square*	*F*	*Sig.*
Type of Investor and Information Bias	Between Groups	71.465	6	11.911	30.071	.000
	Within Groups	116.055	293	.396		
Total		187.520	299			

Table 3
Type of Investor and Over-Confidence

Type of Investor	*Over-Confidence*			*Total*
	Low	*Moderate*	*High*	
Risk Avoiders	57(57.0) (79.2)	23(23.0)(38.3)	20(20.0)(11.9)	100(100)(33.3)
Risk Neutralists	5(4.5)(6.9)	20(17.9)(33.3)	87(77.7)(51.8)	112(100)(37.3)
Risk Takers	10(11.4)(13.9)	17(19.3)(28.3)	61(69.3)(36.3)	88(100)(29.3)
Total	72(24.0)(100)	60(20.0)(100)	168(56.0)(100)	300(100)(100)

There are several dimensions to confidence. Self-Confidence gives more courage and assertiveness to take bold decisions in critical situations which results in success for many, in life and business, hence it is viewed as a positive trait. Although Confidence is often appreciated, it is not the only factor for success. Sometimes, the investors over estimate their predictive skills and knowledge, as they are found to be more analytical, they tend to believe that they can overbeat the market. Studies have shown that one side effect of investor overconfidence is excessive trading (Allen and Evans 2005)[10]; resulting in unexpected losses. Overconfidence was exhibited at a level of 77 percent in Risk Neutralists Investors, consistent with the works of Tversky (1990)[11], Wood (1996), Gervais et al. (2001a, 2001b)[12] and Allen and Evans (2005) who observed that people often interpret their success to be the result of their skills.

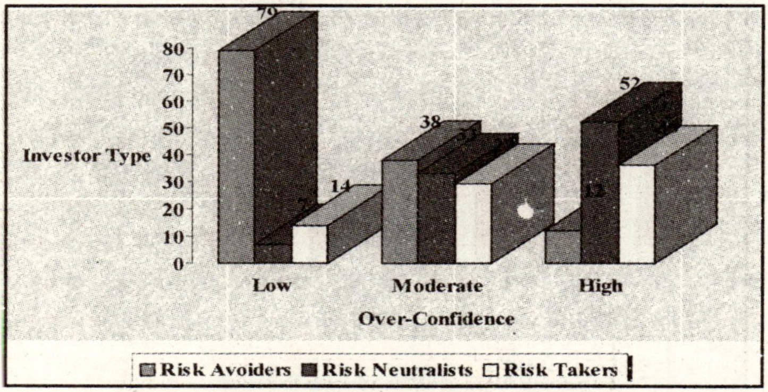

Figure 3: Over-Confidence with Nature of Investor

The F value from the ANOVA Table 4, is 15.64 and the significance value is less than .01, hence deduced that the variables Nature of Investor and Over confidence has significant relationship.

Types of Investors and Discharge-Effect Bias

The discharge Effect bias predicts that investors sell winners too early and ride losers too long (Shefrin and Statman, 1985)[13]. Such behaviour complies with Kahneman and Tversky's

Table 4
ANOVA

		Sum of Squares	*df*	*Mean Square*	*F*	*Sig.*
Type of Investor and Over Confidence	Between Groups	45.491	6	7.582	15.641	.000
	Within Groups	142.029	293	.485		
Total		187.520	299			

(1979)[14] prospect theory suggesting that investors are averse to realize their losses. More specifically, under prospect theory investors assess potential losses and gains using an S- shaped value function quantifying gains and losses rather than levels of wealth as in standard expected utility theory.

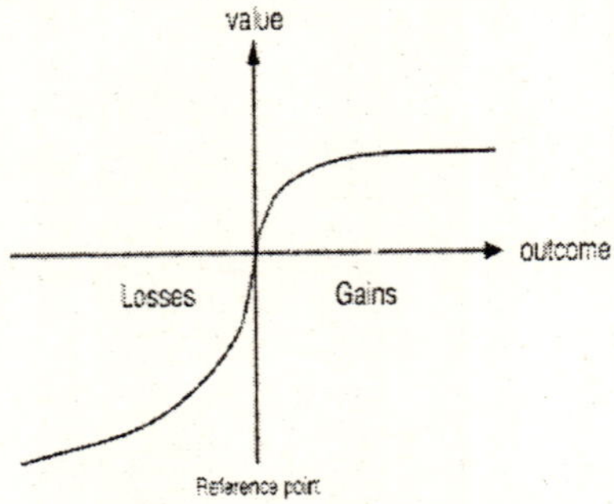

Figure 4: Prospect Theory Value Function**

In other words, the value function (Fig. 4) displays concavity in the domain of gains and convexity in the domain of losses and is steeper for losses than for gains (i.e. loss aversion). From the Table 5, The discharge effect Bias is found to be very low for the Risk Neutralists investor compared with other two. High level of Discharge Effect biasness of 24 percent is found in Risk Takers investors. In a study conducted by Jan Annaert, Dries Heyman, Michèle Vanmaele, Sofieke Van Osselaer, (2007)[15], it was found that the Institutional traders seem to take more rational decisions than individual investors. Moreover, fund managers are not prone to the disposition bias and seem to cut losses early.

Discharge Effect Bias existence has been confirmed by a large number of empirical investigations, by Ferris et al. (1988), Odean (1998), Barber and Odean (1999), Grinblatt and Keloharju (2001), Boebel and Taylor (2000), Barber et al. (2003), Garvey and Murphy (2004), Kaustia (2004a), Frino et al. (2004), Shu et al. (2005), Locke and Onayev (2005), among others[16].

In this study the Risk Takers take higher risk for immediate gains by selling the winners and hold on the losing stock expecting it to rise, and finally end up in heavy losses on losing stock.

Table 5
Type of Investor with Discharge Effect Bias

Type of Investor	Discharge Effect Bias			Total
	Low	Moderate	High	
Risk Avoiders	78(78.0)(32.4)	12(12.0)(42.9)	10(10.0)(32.3)	100(100)(33.3)
Risk Neutralists	110(98.2)(45.6)	2(1.8)(7.1)	0(0.0)(0.0)	112(100)(37.3)
Risk Takers	53(60.2)(22.0)	14(15.9)(50.0)	21(23.9)(67.7)	88(100)(29.3)
Total	241(80.3)(100)	28(9.3)(100)	31(10.3)(100)	300(100)(100)

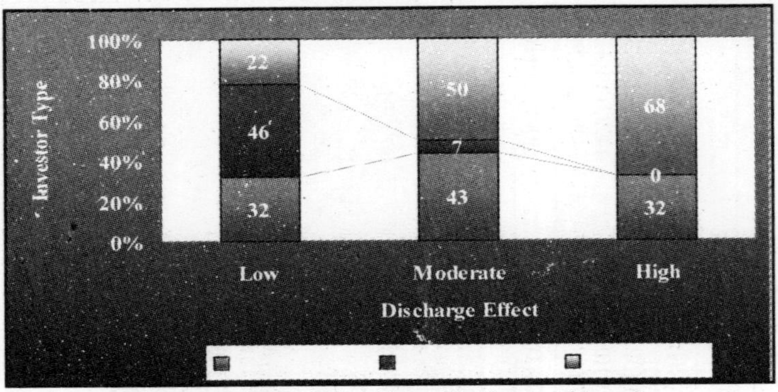

Figure 5: Discharge Effect Bias with Nature of Investor

The ANOVA Table 6 has a significance level of .005 which is less than 1 percent, hence concluded that the two variables Discharge Bias and Nature of Investor have a significant relationship.

Types of Investors and Mindset Bias

Mindset Bias is too conservative extrapolation of current data. It connotes the common human tendency to rely too heavily or 'anchor' on one piece of information while making decisions. And when presented with new information the investors are reluctant or too slow too change from the anchored historical observation. For example, buying a fallen stock is considered a purchase at a cheaper price, so that increase of the stock price to the previously observed level will be the expected gains. This mindset bias impacts many financial decisions. This buy-price anchor leads to odd behaviors like selling your winners too soon and holding on to your losers too long which is the disposition effect discussed previously.

The Mindset Bias level is too high for Risk Avoiders and very low for Risk Takers followed by Risk Neutralists. A moderate level of this bias is found on both Risk Avoiders and Risk Neutralists. These findings concurred with those of Lebaron (1999) and Evans (2002) that investors assumed that current prices, earnings or expectations were correct, and would recur in future. The study conducted in Nairobi Stock

Table 6
ANOVA

		Sum of Squares	*df*	*Mean Square*	*F*	*Sig.*
Type of Investor and Discharge Effect Bias	Between Groups	8.056	3	2.685	4.429	.005
	Within Groups	179.464	296	.606		
Total		187.520	299			

Table 7
Type of Investor with Mindset Bias

Type of Investors	*Mindset Bias*			
	Low	*Moderate*	*High*	*Total*
Risk Avoiders	1(1.0)(1.0)	30(30.0)(34.1)	69(69.0)(62.7)	100(100)(33.3)
Risk Neutralists	46(41.1)(45.1)	43(38.4)(48.9)	23(20.5)(20.9)	112(100)(37.3)
Risk Takers	55(62.5)(53.9)	15(17.0)(17.0)	18(20.5)(16.4)	88(100)(29.3)
Total	102(34.0)(100)	88(29.3)(100)	110(36.7)(100)	300(100)(100)

Exchange on Institutional Investors proved that Anchoring featured prominently, more so in benchmarking against the purchase price.[17]

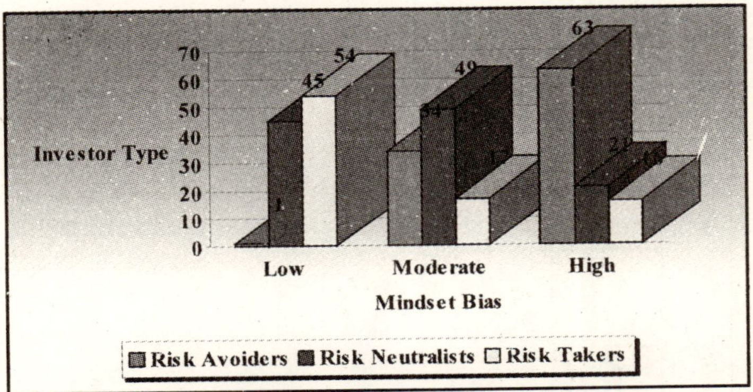

Figure 6: Type of Investor and Mindset Bias

The F value is 38.87 and the significant level is less than 1 percent. The ANOVA Table 8 shows a significant relationship between Mindset Bias and Investor type.

Types of Investors and Spill-Over Enthusiasm

In the midst of the stock market turbulence, after a steep fall in the stock market from January 2008 onwards, was due to the exacerbation of the Spill-Over enthusiasm or herd behavior of investors. The stock market trends and reversals always begin and end with periods of frenzied buying (bubbles–upward movement of market) or panic selling (crashes–downward movement) in a tremendous pace, due to this herd mentality of investors depicted as irrational behavior (Robert Schiller, 2000),[18] without weighing the merits of a particular situation. The study reveals a higher level of this behavior found in Risk Avoiders, lower level in Risk Takers and moderate in Risk Neutralists, shown in Table 9.

The buying and selling decisions were found most frequently (57% each) affected by the trading behavior of other institutional investors at the NSE. These findings are consistent with studies done by De Long et al. (1990), Bikhchandani et al. (1992) and Caparrelli et al. (2004) who argued that

Table 8
ANOVA

		Sum of Squares	*df*	*Mean Square*	*F*	*Sig.*
Type of Investor and Mindset Bias	Between Groups	64.723	4	16.181	38.871	.000
	Within Groups	122.797	295	.416		
	Total	187.520	299			

Table 9
Nature of Investor with Spill-Over Enthusiasm

Type of Investors	*Spill-Over Enthusiasm*			
	Low	*Moderate*	*High*	*Total*
Risk Avoiders	45(45)(28.7)	7(7.0)(11.1)	48(48.0)(60.0)	100(100)(33.3)
Risk Neutralists	55(49.1)(35.0)	27(24.1)(42.9)	30(26.8)(37.5)	112(100)(37.3)
Risk Takers	57(64.8)(36.3)	29(33.0)(46.0)	2(2.3)(2.5)	88(100)(29.3)
Total	157(52.3)(100)	63(21.0)(100)	80(26.7)(100)	300(100)(100)

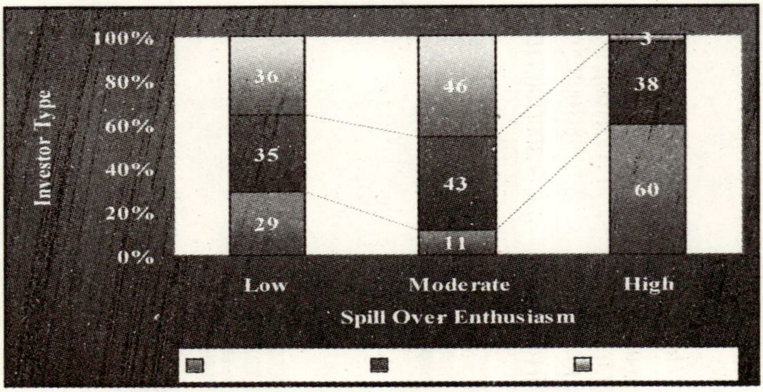

Figure 7: Type of Investor and Spill-Over Enthusiasm

institutional investors simply follow the leaders under peer pressure exhibiting institutional-herding behavior[19]. The relationship between the types of investors and spill over enthusiasm is shown in Figure 7.

The ANOVA Table 10, shows F value of 30.28 at a significance level of less than 1 percent, depicting that the variables Nature of Investor and Spill Over Enthusiasm Bias have significant relationship.

Types of Investors and Situational Reaction Bias

The empirical finding of Investor sentiment on *underreaction* of stock prices to news such as earnings announcements, and *overreaction* of stock prices to a series of good or bad news (Barberis, Andrei Shleifer and Vishny, 1998)[20] found that the investors use the prevalence of past trend reversals as an indicator of the likelihood of future reversals. This behaviour is ridden by corporate announcements or changes in government policies or global economic crisis causing an exuberance in buying or panic selling.

This behaviour is observed at a higher level with the Risk Avoiders investor, lower level with Risk Takers and moderate with Risk Neutralists. Mindset Bias primarily can lead investors to expect a share to continue to trade in a defined range or to expect a company's earnings to be in line with historical trends, leading to possible situational reaction

Table 10
ANOVA

		Sum of Squares	*df*	*Mean Square*	*F*	*Sig.*
Type of Investor with Spill Over Enthusiasm Bias	Between Groups	44.042	3	14.681	30.287	.000
	Within Groups	143.478	296	.485		
Total		187.520	299			

biasness to trend changes. Table 11 and Figure 8 shows the relationship between Types of Investors and situational reaction bias.

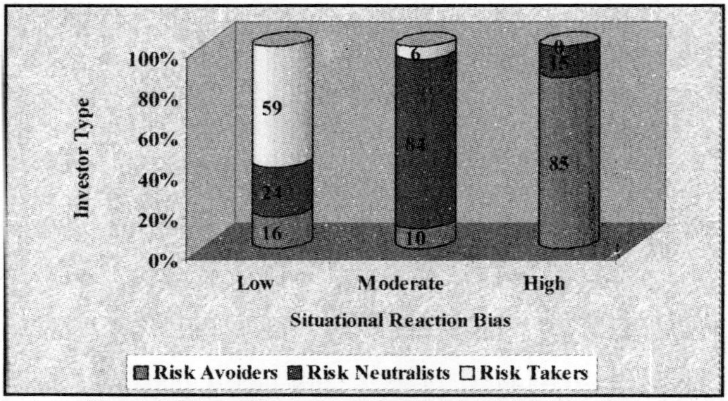

Figure 8: Type of Investor with Situational Reaction Bias

The variables Over or Under reaction and Nature of investors are found to have significant relationship, for the F value 61.31 from the ANOVA Table 12, since the significance level is less than 1 percent.

Types of Investors and Peripheral and Pre-judged Bias

Pre-Judged bias is one of the most pernicious memory biases. Investors think that they had predicted that it would happen

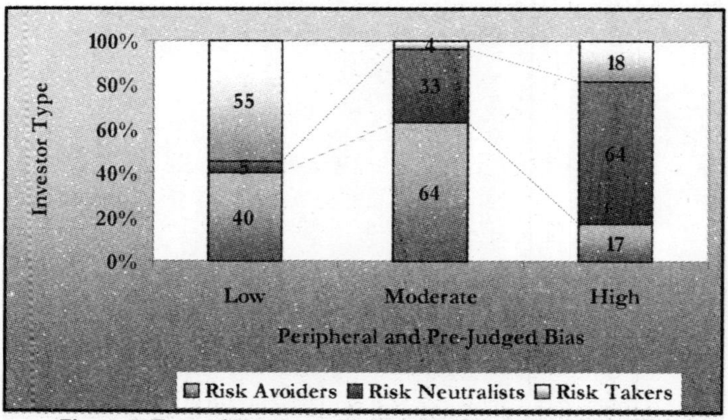

Figure 9: Type of Investor with Peripheral and Pre-Judged Bias

Table 11
Type of Investor with Situational Reaction Bias

Type of Investors	*Situational Reaction Bias*			*Total*
	Low	*Moderate*	*High*	
Risk Avoiders	23(23)(16.4)	8(8)(10.1)	69(69)(85.2)	100(100)(33.3)
Risk Neutralists	34(30.4)(24.3)	66(58.9)(83.5)	12(10.7)(14.8)	112(100)(37.3)
Risk Takers	83(94.3)(59.3)	5(5.7)(6.3)	0(0.0)(0.0)	88(100)(29.3)
Total	140(46.7)(100)	79(26.3)(100)	81(27.0)(100)	300(100)(100)

Table 12
ANOVA

		Sum of Squares	*df*	*Mean Square*	*F*	*Sig.*
Nature of Investors * Over/Under-Reaction	Between Groups	85.126	4	21.281	61.313	.000
	Within Groups	102.394	295	.347		
Total		187.520	299			

Table 13
Type of Investor with Peripheral and Pre-Judged Bias

Type of Investors	*Peripheral and Pre-Judged Bias*			*Total*
	Low	*Moderate*	*High*	
Risk Avoiders	43(43.0)(40.2)	33(33.0)(63.5)	24(24.0)(17.0)	100(100)(33.3)
Risk Neutralists	5(4.5)(4.7)	17(15.2)(32.7)	90(80.4)(63.8)	112(100)(37.3)
Risk Takers	59(67.0)(55.1)	2(2.3)(3.8)	27(30.7)(19.1)	88(100)(29.3)
Total	107(35.7)(100)	52(17.3)(100)	141(47.0)(100)	300(100)(100)

in advance, which in reality it is not so. This behavioral bias prevents people from learning from their mistakes[21]. Kahneman(2000) refers the hindsight bias in his research study as "Prescriptive Analysis" which encourages investors to believe that they "predicted" the future because, after the fact, they "knew" it before it happened. Peripheral bias or recency bias is a predisposition for investors to recall and emphasize recent events and observations. During the downfall of the stock market in 2008, many investors were holding the stocks they had bought at higher prices presuming that there would be regain in the prices, instead of selling at lesser loss. The result was heavy losses on sharp decline of stocks. This biasness is observed at a higher level in Risk Neutralists and lower level for Risk Avoiders and Risk Takers.

The variables Peripheral and Pre Judged Bias and Type of investors are found to have significant relationship, for the F value 14.50 from the ANOVA Table 14, since the significance level is less than 1 percent.

Types of Investors and Gambler's Fallacy

Gamblers' fallacy arises when people inappropriately predict that a trend will reverse. This may lead investors to anticipate the end of a run of good (or poor) market returns. In the gambler's fallacy, an individual erroneously believes that the onset of a certain random event is less likely to happen

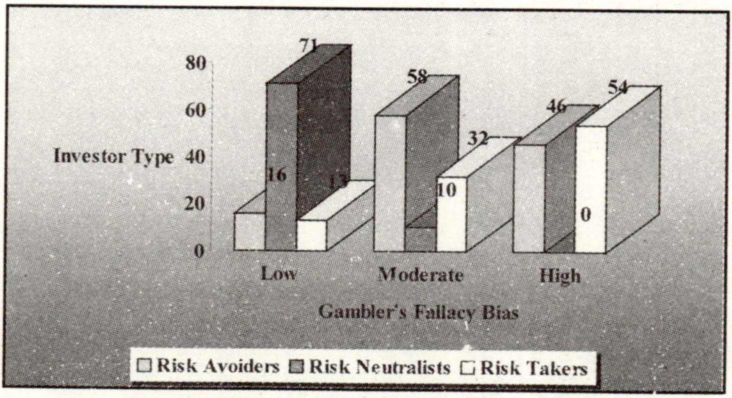

Figure 10: Type of Investor with Gambler's Fallacy

Table 14
ANOVA

		Sum of Squares	*df*	*Mean Square*	*F*	*Sig.*
Type of Investors and Peripheral and Pre-Judged Bias	Between Groups	24.031	3	8.010	14.503	.000
	Within Groups	163.489	296	.552		
Total		187.520	299			

Table 15
Type of Investor with Gambler's Fallacy

Type of Investors	*Gambler's Fallacy*			*Total*
	Low	*Moderate*	*High*	
Risk Avoiders	24(24.0)(16.0)	34(34.0)(57.6)	42(42.0)(46.2)	100(100)(33.3)
Risk Neutralists	106(94.6)(70.7)	6(5.4)(10.2)	0(0.0)(0.0)	112(100)(37.3)
Risk Takers	20(22.7)(13.3)	19(21.6)(32.2)	49(55.7)(53.8)	88(100)(29.3)
Total	150(50.0)(100)	59(19.7)(100)	91(30.3)(100)	300(100)(100)

following an event or a series of events. Investors or traders easily fall prey to the gambler's fallacy. For example, some investors believe that they should liquidate a position after it has gone up in a series of subsequent trading sessions because they don't believe that the position is likely to continue going up. Conversely, other investors might hold on to a stock that has fallen in multiple sessions because they view further declines as "improbable". Just because a stock has gone up on six consecutive trading sessions does not mean that it is less likely to go up on during the next session.

This attitude is found to be high with the Risk Avoiders and Risk Takers investors and zero level for Risk Neutralists investors.

The ANOVA Table 16, shows F value of 4.337 at a significance level of less than 1 percent, depicting that the variables Nature of Investor and Gambler's Fallacy have significant relationship.

In the Table, the behavioral factors have a statistically significant relationship with the Average Earned Return except for Discharge effect Bias and Situational Reaction bias. The Earned Return of the investors under study, seem to be not affected by these behavior at a great extent.

Association Among Variables and Its Influence

A further attempt is also made in this chapter to study the degree of association among the eight biases and its influence on the types of investors. This analysis may establish the correlation among variables and the explanatory power of the variables. For this purpose the data was subjected to regression analysis. All the eight variables taken into study was referred with the dependent variable 'Types of Investors', applying the Regression Model to assess the multiple correlation among the factors.

In the Table 17, the Model summary 'R' stands for Multiple Correlation showing the degree of association among the variables which is 82.5% and *R Square* is the influence of the independent variable on dependant variable which is 68.1%. The remaining $1 - R^2$ is the unexplained variation. From the

Table 16
ANOVA

		Sum of Squares	df	Mean Square	F	Sig.
Nature of Investors * Gambler's Fallacy	Between Groups	7.895	3	2.632	4.337	.005
	Within Groups	179.625	296	.607		
Total		187.520	299			

Table 17
Regression : Model Summary

Model	R	R^2	Adjusted R^2	Std. Error of the Estimate
1	.825	.681	.673	.453

(a) Predictors: (Constant), Gambler's Fallacy, Disposition Bias, Anchoring Bias, Over/Under-Reaction, Recency/Hindsight Bias, Contagious Enthusiasm, Over Confidence, Availability Bias
(b) Dependent Variable: Basic Nature of Investors

regression Analysis it is concluded that all the factors have a high positive correlation of 82.5 percent.

The purpose of regression is to establish cause and effect relationship to predict the future values for variables. Table 18, discloses the influences of independent variables on dependant variables, where in this study, the dependant

Table 18
ANOVA

	Sum of Squares	df	Mean Square	F	Sig.
Regression	127.777	8	15.972	77.798	.000
Residual	59.743	291	.205		
Total	187.520	299			

Table 19
Coefficients of the Variables Identified

Model	Unstandardized Coefficients B	Unstandardized Coefficients Std. Error	Standardized Coefficients Beta	t	Sig. Std. Error
1 (Constant)	2.611	.283		9.216	.000
Information bias	.255	.043	.259	5.960	.000
Overconfidence	.096	.041	.102	2.368	.019
Discharge Effect Bias	.288	.045	.235	6.423	.000
Mindset Bias	-.265	.040	-.282	-6.651	.000
Spill Over Enthusiasm Bias	.086	.040	.100	1.673	.000
Situational Reaction Bias	-.397	.044	-.419	-8.942	.000
Peripheral and Pre-Judged Bias	-.209	.037	-.239	-5.673	.000
Gambler's Fallacy	-.002	.038	-.003	-.061	.952

a Dependent Variable: *Type of Investors*

variable is the "Type of Investors" and the Independent variables are the 8 behavioral factors identified from the analysis. The variables has a significant value less than .01 and is observed that the relationship exists between the dependent and independent variables.

The purpose of coefficient Table 19 given above, is to see whether individually the independent variables are statistically significant against the dependant variable. In the given table all the significant values of all the variables are significant except factor 8. By looking into the standardized coefficient data, the researcher can come to a conclusion that except for the Gambler's Fallacy all other variables have a significant value of less than .01% hence deduced that the variables 1 to 7 has a significant relationship with the Basic nature of Investors.

Conclusion

The findings of this chapter are summed up as follows

- Each of the eight heuristic behavioral biases individually influence the three different types of investors. This is evident from the ANOVA test, revealing significant relationship in all the eight biases with the types of investors. Hence the null hypothesis is rejected.
- There is association among all the eight variables and the 'R' value explains 82.5% of relationship among all the eight variables. There is a high positive correlation among variables.
- The extent of influence of all eight variables taken together (as independent variables) on the type of investors (taken as dependent variable) account for 68.1% which is considered as significant.
- Examination of standardized coefficient data (beta) for all the eight variables reveal that except for Gambler's fallacy, all the seven variables show significant relationship with the type of investors.

On the whole, it is clear that the heuristic biases/ factors have influence on the types of investors at varying degrees, which in turn affects their average rate of returns in their stock market investments.

Footnotes

1. Peter J Klein, (1998), " Getting started in Security Analysis", *John Wiley & Sons*, 190-92
2. Paul Krugman, "Seven Habits of Highly Defective Investors", *Fortune 500 magazine*, (Dec. 29, 1997)
3. John W Sctt & Jean S Arbeiter, (1998), " Mind over Money: Match your Personality to a winning Financial strategy", *Little Brown Publishers*.
4. Thomas Bailard, David Biehl and Ronald Kaiser, (1986), " Personal Money Management", *Chicago Science Research Associate*, 5th edn.
5. Kathleen Gurney, (1988), " Your Money Personality: What It is and How you can profit from it", *Doubleday Books Publishers* .
6. Micheal M.Pompian, (2006),"Behavioral Finance and Wealth Management – How to build Optimal Portfolios that account for Investor Biases", *John Wiley Sons*.
7. Ellsberg Daniel, (1961), "Risk Ambiguity and the Savage Axioms", *Quarterly Journal of Economics*, Vol. 75, No4, 643- 669.
8. Thaler, Richard H, (May, 1994), "Psychology and Savings Policies", *American Economic Review*, Vol.84, No2, 186- 192
9. Barberis, N.,(2000), "Investing for the Long run when returns are predictable", *Journal of Finance*, Vol.55, 225- 264.
10. W. David Allen; Dorla A. Evans, (2005), " Bidding and Over Confidence in Experimental Financial markets", *Journal of Behavioral Finance*, Vol 6, Issue 3, 108 – 120.
11. Tversky, Amos & Thaler, Richard H, (1990), "Anomalies : Preference Reversals", Journal of Economic Perspectives, American Economic Association, Vol. 4, No2, 201-211.
12. Gervais Simon and Odean Terrance, (2001), "Learning to be Overconfident", *Review of Financial studies*, Issue 14, 1 -27.
13. Statman Meir, (1985) "The Disposition to sell Winners too early and Ride Losers Too long: Theory and Evidence", Journal of Finance, Vol. 60, No 3.
14. Kahneman, Daniel, and Amos Tversky, (1979), " Prospect Theory: An analysis of Decision under Risk", Econometrica, Vol.67, 263-291
    ** source : Kahneman and Tversky, Shafir Eldar, (1979), " Preference, Belief and Similarity", MIT press, 545 - 567
15. Jan Annaert, Dries Heyman, Michele Vanmaele, Sofieke Van Osselaer, "Disposition bias and Overconfidence in institutional trades", Working paper, (2007).
16. Odean Terrance, (1998), "Are Investors reluctant to realize their losses", *The Journal of Finance*, Vol. 53, No.5. ; Mark Grinblatt and Matti Keloharju, (2001), " What makes Investors Trade", *Journal of Finance*, Vol.56, No.2, 589 -616; Garvey Ryan and Murphy Anthony, (2004), " Are Professional Traders too slow to realize their losses", *Financial Analysts Journal*, Vol.

60, No 4, 35-43.; Barber B M and Odean T., (1999), " The courage of misguided convictions", *Financial Analysts Journal*, Vol 55, No.6, 41-55.; Pete Locke and Onayev Zhan, (2005), " Trade Duration: Information and Trade Disposition", *Financial Review*, Vol.40, No 1 ; Markku Kaustia, (2004), " Market-wide impact of the disposition effect" Evidence from IPO trading volume", *Journal of Financial Markets*, Vol.7, No.2, 207- 235

17. LeBaron, Blake, (1999), "Technical Trading Rule Profitability and Foreign Exchange Intervention", Journal of International Economics, Issue 49, 125-143.
18. Robert Schiller, (2001), " Irrational Exuberance", International Journal of Forecasting, Vol 17, Issue 2, 295 -297 .
19. Robert B Barsky and J Bradford DeLong, (1990), " Bull and Bear Markets in the Twentieth century", *Journal of Economic History*, Vol 50, Issue 2, 1-17.; S Bikhchanani and S Sharma, (2001), "Herd Behavior in Financial Markets: A Review", IMF Staff Papers, Vol. 47, 279-310.; Nelson Maina Waweru, Evelyne Munyoki, Enrico Uliana (2008), "The Effects of Behavioral factors in Investment decision making: A survey of institutional investors operating at the Nairobi Stock Exchange", *International Journal of Business and Emerging Markets*, Vol.1, Issue 1, 24-37
20. Nicholas Barberis, Andrei Shleifer and R Vishny, (1998), " A Model of Investor Sentiment", *Journal of Financial Economics*, Vol 49, 307-343.
21. Richard L Peterson, (2007), " Inside the Investor's Brain – The Power of Mind over Money", John Wiley & Sons, 266-269.

8

Summary and Conclusion

"*The investor's worst enemy is likely to be himself*"- Benjamin Graham[1]. The steep fall in Sensex and Nifty in the year 2008, at the event of global economic slowdown, causing a recessionary trend, and people comparing with the Great Depression,1929, market experts and analysts too were unable to predict how the economy would move in the year 2009. The rally of bull market in 2006 –'07, followed by the bearish trend in 2008, seem to worry the world markets and India being not an exception, the measures and offer of various fiscal stimulus packages* of the government/s, to revive the economy and pump in liquidity, added positive sentiments and hence markets seemed to have stabilized in December 2008. Thus bringing to halt the irrational behaviour of the markets. In this rally fundamentally sound stocks rallied more than others and the expectation was whether this new-found rationality will lead to the resumption of bull market again in 2009.

Investors in this period, have seen their wealth, especially in shares erode faster than they would have imagined. What had began as a global liquidity glut four years ago (2004 –'05), has eventually ended as a liquidity crisis in 2008, where opportunities for investments were limited and fraught with risk. These haphazard movements in the markets are primarily integrated with the market sentiments caused by the irrational behaviour of the investors. The research study was intended to analyse these behavioral biases strongly exhibited by the investors, causing a major setback in the economy as a whole and fleecing the wealth of the individual investor.

The specific objectives include the demographic factors and investment profile of the investors in capital market, to understand their preferable choices of their investment. Apart from these objectives the research also attempted to measure the heuristics attitude and explain the relationship between these measures and the overall returns earned by them. The research design was descriptive and explanatory in nature.

The researcher selected the institutions and organizations involving in stock trading operations within Bangalore city. The reason was that, Bangalore being a metropolitan city is a place of heterogeneous culture from various parts of India, a major portion of its population included Knowledge - based, high- income group, attracted to Capital market during the bull trend from 2005 to 2007. There was a tremendous growth in the number of stock traders and trading firms during this period, to encash on the uptrend market.

The Summary of Findings is presented below, based on the specific objectives of the study:

The personal factors of the investors were considered to be important for the study as each factor had considerable contribution towards the behavioral attitude in capital market investment. The sample consisted of around three-fifth of respondents above 40 years of age (64%) ; one –fourth were between 20 to 30 years (26%) and one-tenth were between the age of 30 and 40 years (9.4%). Those within the age group of 20 to 30 years included students constituting nearly 15 percent of the total sample.

Education plays a major role in this study. Around one-third (34.7%) were having Post-graduate qualification ; one-fourth (26.7%) were professionals ; another one-fourth (25%) were Graduates and the remaining had only educated at secondary and higher secondary level.

The distribution of the sample based on the occupational category, had more than one-third (38%) working in private companies, one-sixth (15.7%) from public companies; around one-tenth (13%) were self-employed and (10%) in Business.

More than one-third (37%) of the investors had less than five years of experience in stock market investments. Less than one-fourth of them (ie.21.7%) had an experience between 5 to 10 years and another around one-fourth (22%) had counted an experience above 15 years.

The tenure or period of investment chosen by the investors constituted, more than half (62.7%) in short-term; less than one-fourth (ie.,20%) in speculative trading; 13.7% choice were long-term and 3.6% were in intermediate or medium-term category.

The category of investors had majority (72%) of the respondents being retail investors; 17% intermediaries; 8% of High Networth Individuals (HNIs) and 3% of Fund Managers.

More than half of the investors' (55.7%) total Value of Investment was less than Rs. 5 lakh; one-third (32.7%) of then had an investment value within Rs. 10 and 15 lakh; and 8.3% were having an investment above Rs.15 lakh.

Most of the respondents (39.7%) had their investments based on 'Market reaction' for particular stocks; around one-third (33.7%) of the respondents' choice were 'Industry' based and 8.3% had chosen their stocks based on the 'Management Team' leading the company.

The respondents were required to classify themselves under any one of the three types of investors based on their Risk appetite. It was found that more than one-third (37.3%) of them have identified themselves as Risk-Neutralists; another 33.3% have suggested that they belong to Risk-Avoiders category and the remaining 29.3% have opined that they fall under the category of Risk-Takers.

Most of the respondents (44.3%) have suggested that they would prefer to avoid 'over-reacting to the fear of uncertain times, both good or bad'; 35% have felt that they wouldn't like to trust on their own intuitions in investment decisions and around one-sixth (15.7%) have consented that they don't depend on Fundamental or Technical analysis in their decisions on stock picks.

More than half (58.3%) of the respondents have expected a market return of more than 50%. The general expectation of any investor used to be much higher than the reality, which is an illusion about the capital market attracting more number of people into this arena. Only a one-fourth of the sample (18.7%) have agreed their expected return from market is less than 30%.

Unlike the expected market return the actual returns seem to vary. One-third (33%) of the respondents have expressed that they have earned a return of 20% to 30%; another one-fourth have earned a return below 20% and only one-sixth (17%) have been able to earn an average return of above 40%.

The choice of constructing a portfolio or choosing specific stocks are widely based on the decisions of the investors, either intuitive or influenced by others. Based on the level of risk appetite of the investors, the choice of stock picks might also vary. It was found that majority (70%) of the respondents under study, have taken decisions on their own; and 22.3% have opted to decide on their stock picks taking the suggestions from their friends or peer group.

Most of the respondents have justified that they rely upon their own instincts about the market along with the technical analysis deployed for picking stocks. Remaining one-third have consented that they would take the advice from technical analysts.

The data analysis, have shown that Risk Takers are more in number in the age group of 40 and above and risk-Avoiders seem to be high within the age group of 20 to 30 years. Therefore it can be concluded that, higher the age, greater the risk taken whereas lesser the age, the level of risk taking capacity is low.

It was observed from the Two-way analysis , Education exhibits the tendency of the investors in taking risk. Majority of the respondents qualified as Post-Graduates and Professionals were observed to be Risk-Neutral. And Less educated investors (84.2%) were found to be Risk-Avoiders. Hence it can be concluded that more qualified investors tend to be more Objective in taking decisions and lesser the education level, they seek assistance from others either from analysts or friends and peer group, so as to avoid the risk of losing money.

Taking the occupational category as a correlation variable with the nature of investors, it was found that the students (89%) were cautious in taking decisions and tried to avoid risk to the maximum possible. Those working in private concerns, are found to be capable of taking higher risk in capital market investments. And those who were in business (76.7%) and self-employed entrepreneurs (48.7%), were observed to be risk-neutral.

It was observed from the data that higher the Experience (77.6%), greater is the Risk Tolerance and become Risk Neutral due to their longer association with capital Market. The new entrants having lesser experience (60.4%) about the nuances of the capital market are prone to be Risk-Avoiders. Those within a medium term (64.9%) period of association are found to be Risk Takers.

Short- term investors have been found to be more or less dispersed equally among all three categories of investors. One-third of the speculative investors who are more inclined towards day-trading with an urge of earning immediate gains are observed to be Risk-Neutral. This attitude can be due to their experience facing both the losses and gains in day-to day basis, making them immune to risk. One-fourth of the speculative investors seem to be Risk Avoiders also. Hence, can be concluded from the data that short-term investors take higher risk than other long term or intermediate investors. This behavior can be attributed due to the desire of earning quick profits within a short span of time.

Nearly 92 percent of them whose investment value was greater than Rs.15 lakh, were from Risk Neutral category. Such large investments are normally from the Institutional Investors or HNIs, hence, it can be concluded that, they are neither Risk Takers, who generally prefer investments in blue chip companies, nor they avoid risk. The investors with less value of investment (40.7%), are small investors, found to be Risk-Averse, who try to avoid taking risk. The remaining investors with an investment less than Rs.10 lakh, were Risk Takers, intending to take more risk due to greediness of earning immediate profits.

Most of the investors (69.6%) have reacted on the advice or suggestions taken from their family members, fall under the Risk Neutral category. Around 33.3 percent have taken risk of deciding on their own.. But one-third of the respondents (35.8%) have taken the opinion from their friends and peer group.

The Fund Managers have a higher Risk Taking behaviour. The Fund Managers are pressurized to take crucial decisions, at the same time to take wise decisions during challenging situations, like a downfall market or a bubble crash, when they are compelled to take risk. Majority of the HNIs (62.5%) were found to be Risk Neutral. The value of investment being large balancing with a minimum risk of loss, makes them Risk Neutral.

To explain the heuristic behaviour of investors in stock market, this study has identified the following factors;

1. Information Bias
2. Over-Confidence Bias
3. Discharge Effect Bias
4. Mindset Bias
5. Spill - Over Enthusiasm Bias
6. Situational Reaction Bias
7. Peripheral and Pre-Judged Bias
8. Gambler's Fallacy

The predominant eight factors have been put to further analysis to find out if they have any influence on the types of investors and also on their average returns earned from the investments in stock market.

Association of Personal and Investment Factors with the Earned Returns

The association of personal and investment factors with their Earned Returns were analysed from a Two-Way analysis.

- Analyzing the age of investors with their Earned Returns the results were that, those respondents in the age group of 30 and 40 years, have earned good returns better than those in the other age group. This is supported by the result of the mean value being the highest for this age group. The statistical test using ANOVA showed that the age of the respondents has a significant relationship with the Earned Returns.

- The data revealed that higher the level of education, higher the returns. In other words, education contributes to a greater extent in increasing the returns on the investment in stock market, according to the data collected. It was found that the ANOVA result approved a significant relationship between Education and Earned Returns.
- Experience in any job or profession adds more wisdom and knowledge in the field whoever is associated with. The data reveals that higher the experience in the field of Investment in Stock market, higher the returns earned. The ANOVA result showed the variables Experience in Stock market and Earned Return is having statistically significant relationship.
- A key step in investment planning is defining the time horizon, or the length of time to work on the investment goals. It can be concluded from the data, during the boom period of stock market, more number of speculative and short-term investments has reaped good gains for the investors than the intermediate and the long term investors. The result also showed significant relationship between the two variables.
- From the analysis of the data collected, it has been concluded that higher investment has given higher returns and those with lesser amount of investment have earned minimum returns. Hence it is deduced that higher investment value has fetched handful of gains. The outcome of ANOVA resulted in deducing that Earned Returns has a significant relationship with the value of Investment made.
- An expected return is a projected return that already averages out mathematically the probabilities of gains

and losses. The Expected Returns are usually high when compared to the Actual Earned Returns. Though the Expected and Earned returns are inversely related, the Earned Returns are observed to be considerably satisfactory from the above data analysis, and this seem to be reliable due to the upward movement of the market, during the period of data collection. The ANOVA observed significant relationship between the two variables.

- In case of Risk Takers and Risk Neutral investors, it was found that above 50 percent of the investors were earning more than 30 percent returns as compared with the Risk Avoiders. This trend is also related to the favourable market movement for the investors, especially for the Risk Takers. ANOVA showed a significant relationship between the two variables.
- The analysis of the data on the returns earned by the investors under varied investment category revealed that the Fund Managers and High Networth Individuals have comparably earned more returns than the retail investors. The retail investors were found to have earned lesser returns and sometimes incurred losses also. ANOVA showed a significant relationship between the two variables.

Investor Type and Heuristic-Driven Biases

Several Behavioral Finance scholars have categorized the investors based on various grounds. The researcher attempted to classify on the risk-taking capacity along with their analytical skills. The Investors were typified as;

1. Risk Avoiders
2. Risk Takers and
3. Risk Neutralists

The attempt made to analyse the relationship between the Types of Investors and the identified Eight Heuristic Biases in the Investor's behavior has exhibited the following results;

Information Biasness and Type of Investor

Heuristics bring *cognitive biases* in the decision making process. They on their turn cause market activity and price distortions. The data analysis reveals that low level of Information Bias was more or less the same among the Risk Neutralists and Risk Takers. But moderate level of Information Bias was more among the Risk Takers than the Risk Avoiders. A high level of Information Bias was found among the Risk Neutralists. This is because the Risk Neutralists found to be more analytical in nature, searching for more and more information for confirming their decisions to be right.

Over Confidence Bias and Type of Investor

It is found from the data, that the level of Over Confidence is low for Risk Avoiders compared with the other two types of investors, and all three investor category have moderate level of Over-Confidence. High Level of Over Confidence is found among the Risk Neutralists.

Discharge Effect Bias and Type of Investor

The discharge effect Bias is found to be very low for the Risk Neutralists investor compared with other two. High level of Discharge Effect biasness of 24 percent is found in Risk Takers investors. In this study the Risk Takers take higher risk for immediate gains by selling the winners and hold on the losing stock expecting it to rise, and finally end up in heavy losses on losing stock.

Mindset Bias and Type of Investor

The study revealed that, Mindset Bias level being too high for Risk Avoiders and very low for Risk Takers followed by Risk Neutralists. A moderate level of this bias is found on both Risk Avoiders and Risk Neutralists. This is because the Risk Avoiders tend to 'anchor' on a certain information and reluctant to change their predetermined mindset, due to avoidance of taking risk.

Spill Over Enthusiasm Bias and Type of Investor

The study reveals a higher level of this behavior found in Risk Avoiders, lower level in Risk Takers and moderate in Risk Neutralists. The Risk Avoiders are most prone to the herd instinct to play safe in their investments which leads their decisions to be biased.

Situational Reaction and Type of Investor

This behavior is observed at a higher level with the Risk Avoiders, lower level with Risk Takers and moderate with Risk Neutralists. This behavior is ridden by corporate announcements or changes in government policies or global economic crisis causing an exuberance in buying or disaster in panic selling. The risk avoiders react more in both the situations and hence take biased decisions.

Peripheral and Pre-Judged Bias and Type of Investor

During the downfall of the stock market in 2008, many investors were holding the stocks they had bought at higher prices presuming that there would be regain in the prices, instead of selling at lesser loss. The result was heavy losses on sharp decline of stocks. This biasness is observed at a higher level among the Risk Neutralists and at a lower level for Risk Avoiders and Risk Takers.

Gambler's Fallacy and Type of Investor

This attitude is found to be high with the Risk Avoiders and Risk Takers and zero level for Risk Neutralists. Just because a stock has gone up on six consecutive trading sessions does not mean that it is less likely to go up on during the next session.

Regression Analysis

All the eight variables taken into study was referred with the Dependent variable 'Type of Investor', applying the Regression model to assess the Multiple Correlation among the factors. From the regression Analysis it is concluded that all the factors have a high positive correlation of 82.5 percent.

Rank Correlation for Prioritizing their Investments in Mutual Funds

It is observed from the analysis, that the top priority to invest among the various alternatives of Mutual Funds, was the 'Aggressive Growth fund', as it gives additional gains from equity investments during the surge in market betting on a GDP of 9 percent during the period 2006-2007. The least preference was given to Long term convertible debentures due to lack of Liquidity and lesser returns considered to be not a preferable investment when the market is booming. Growth and balanced funds were also considered preferable investment choices by the investors.

CONCLUSION

Fear of loss is an invisible nemesis undermining the financial success. This financial fear creates anxiety lingering deep into the investor's mind. The economic decisions of a human being are more emotionally based than rationally based. Several money myths, like Money is Freedom, Money gives Power, It is security, It is Life, It is Love and Happiness , triggers intense emotions like fear, obsession, anxiety, greed etc. which makes difficult to handle even simplest of the financial decisions. It is the preparedness required to understand that Money is not the Master, but to use it as a tool to enhance its value requires patience, lesser attachment, control of mind in making quick money.

Stock Market does not behave in a predictable way. What is interesting about Behavioral Finance, is that the experiments that are conducted try to explain why this happens and if we better understand how we behave and react to things, then we can reshape our world and systems to match that behavior to improve the situation.

Being an investor in the capital market it is required to be smart in taking appropriate direction and also timing of entry and exit. From the study it is evident that decisions of the investors' is based on information gathered from various sources to some extent and is more influenced by their intuition. Hence, it is less of science and more of Arts. Even going by the established studies relating to evaluation of investment decisions like Fundamental Analysis, Technical Analysis and Random Walk Theory, we have an element of subjective factors which cannot be quantified to give a scientific approach to investment decisions. Hence, the psychological or behavioral factors play a vital role in influencing the decisions.

The fundamental theory of investment is that "Higher the risk higher may be the return", but, risk taking ability of an investor depends mainly on his basic traits like behavior, environment, etc. Hence, behavior of the investor has a direct relationship with the nature of investment decisions he takes. Behavioral finance as a study correlates the investors' behavior and his risk taking ability/tendency which in turn decides the return pattern.

The study has beyond doubt established the relationship existing between the heuristic behavioral factors on the investment decisions of the investor. It is rightly concluded that the heuristic biases/factors influence on the types of investors at varying degrees, which in turn affects their average earned returns.

Recommendations for Further Research

Some of the studies recommended for further research may be:

- Forecast errors by Portfolio Managers and novices in forecasts of Risk and Return
- Anomalies in the market in the Indian context, its implications and Rationality
- The impact of Behavioral finance on Stock-Price Volatality
- Market Beating Investment strategies using the Behavioral Finance Principles
- The Implications of Herding Behavior for estimation of Earnings, Risk Assessment and Stock Returns

Footnotes

1. Benjamin Graham , A legendary value investor and one of the fathers of modern security analysis.

* The markets displayed strong buoyancy due to global events such as US Fed cut rate, OPEC meeting, decline in crude oil price, strong FII buying in Indian markets, inflation down at 6.84% (as on 21st December, 2008) and rate cuts by RBI and other commercial banks in India, boosted the market sentiment quite a bit.

Bibliography

Fama, Eugene F. (1970), "Efficient Capital Markets: A Review of Theory and Empirical Work", *Journal of Finance*, Vol.25, No.2, pp 383-417.

Fama, Eugene F. (1991), "Efficient Capital Markets II", *The Journal of Finance*, Vol. 46, No.5, pp. 1575-1617.

Louis Bachelier (1900), "The Theory of Speculation", *Mathematical Finance*, Blackwell Publishers, Vol 10, No. 3, pp. 341-353.

Sharpe, William F. (1964), "Capital Asset Prices - A Theory of Market Equilibrium Under Conditions of Risk". *Journal of Finance* Vol. XIX No.3, pp. 425–42.

Bernartzi, Shlomo and Richard H. Thaler (1999), "Risk Aversion or Myopia? Choices in Repeated Gambles and Retirement Investment", *Management Science,* Vol. 45, No.1, pp. 364-381.

Statman Meir (1985), "The Disposition to Sell Winners Too Early and Ride Losers Too Long: Theory and Evidence", *Journal of Finance*, Vol. XL, No. 3.

Statman Meir (1987), "How Many Stocks Make a Diversified Portfolio?" *Journal of Financial and Quantitative Analysis,*

Robert J Shiller (2000), "Irrational Exuberance", Princeton University Press.

Bernstein, Peter L. (1996), "Against The Gods: The Remarkable Story of Risk", John Wiley & Sons, New York.

Kahneman, D., & Riepe, M. (1998), "Aspects of Investor Psychology: Beliefs, Preferences and Biases Investment Advisors Should Know About", *The Journal of Portfolio Management,* Vol. 24, pp. 52-65.

Kahneman, D., & Tversky, A. (1996), "On the Reality of Cognitive Illusions: A Reply to Gigerenzer's Critique", *Psychological Review,* Vol.103, pp.582-591.

Michael J. Seiler; Clint Tan Chee Leong & Mark Lane (2002), "Explaining Apparent Stock Market Anomalies: Irrational Exuberance or Archetypal Human Psychology?"

Ralph L. Keeney, Howard Raiffa, Richard Meyer (1993), "Decisions with Multiple Objectives: Preferences and Value Trade-Offs", Cambridge University Press.

Fama, Eugene F. (1965), "Random Walks In Stock Market Prices", *Financial Analysts Journal* , Vol.21, No. 5, pp. 55–59.

Maurice G. Kendall and B. Babington Smith (1938), "Randomness and Random Sampling Numbers," Journal of the Royal Statistical Society, Vol. 101:1, pp. 147-166.

Malkiel, Burton G. (1973), "A Random Walk Down Wall Street" W.W. Norton & Company, Inc. pub., 6th edn., pp.45-48.

James Dow and Gary Gorton (1997), "Stock Market Efficiency and Economic Efficiency: Is There a Connection?", *The Journal of Finance*, Vol.LII, No.3, pp.1087 -1127.

Basu, S. (1977), "Investment Performance of Common Stocks in relation to their Price-Earnings Ratio: A Test of the Efficient Market Hypothesis", The Journal of Finance, Vol.32, No.3, pp 663–674.

Maurice Kendall (1953), "The Analysis of Economic Time –Series- Part I : Price", Journal of the Royal Statistical Society, Vol.116, No.1, pp.11–34.

William Goetzmann and Alok Kumar (2004), "Diversification Decisions of Individual Investors and Asset Prices.", pp. 1-58, 14 January.

Susan Thomas (2002), "India's Capital Markets: Have We Come Full Circle?", *Outlook* Magazine, 14 January.

Hersh Shefrin (2005), "A Behavioral Approach to Asset Pricing", *Academic Press Advanced Finance Series,* pp 203-204.

Daniel Kahneman and Amos Tverksy (1979), "Prospect Theory: An Analysis of Decision Under Risk," *Econometrica*, Vol. 47 pp 263-291.

Paul Presson and Victor Benassi (1996), "Illusion of Control", *Journal of Social Behavior and Personality*, Vol. 11, No.3, pp. 493-510.

Nicholas Barberis, Ming Huang and Richard Thaler (2006), "Individual Preferences, Monetary Gambles, and Stock Market

Participation: A Case for Narrow Framing", *American Economic Review* Vol. 96, pp.169-175.

Jon Elster (1999), Alchemies of the Mind: Rationality and The Emotions, Cambridge University Press, pp. 285-287.

John R. Nofsinger (2001), "Investment Madness", Prentice Hall, pp. 13-15.

Hersh Shefrin (2000), "Beyond Greed and Fear: Understanding Behavioral Finance and the Psychology of Investing", *Harvard Business School Press,* pp. 92- 96.

Takemura, K. (1992), "Effect of Decision Time on Framing of Decision: A Case of Risky Choice. Behavior". *Psychologia,* Vol. 35, pp. 180-185.

Takemura, K. (1994), "Influence of Elaboration on the Framing of Decisions", *Journal of Psychology,* Vol. 128, pp. 33–39.

Mary Kynn (2007), "The 'Heuristics and Biases' Bias in Expert Elicitation", Journal of the Royal Statistical Society: Series A (Statistics in Society), Vol.171, Issue 1 , pp. 239-264.

Marco Cipriani & Antonio Guarino (2002), "Herding and Price Convergence in a Laboratory Financial Market".

Didier Sornette (2003), "Why Stock Market Crash- Critical Events in Complex Financial Systems", Princeton University Press, 7-9.

Kent Daniel, David Hirshleifer, Avanidhar Subrahmanyam (2002), "Investor Psychology and Security Market Under-and Overreactions", *The Journal of Finance,* Volume 53, Issue 6, pp. 24-29.

Hogarth, Robin M, Einhorn, Hillel J. (1992), 'Order Effects in Belief Updating: Belief-Adjustment Model', *Journal of Cognitive Psychology,* Vol. 24 Issue 1, pp. 15–18.

Richard Thaler (1999), "Mental Accounting Matters", *Journal of Behavioral Decision Making,* Volume 12, Issue 3, pp. 183-206, July.

Hersh Shefrin (2002), "Behavioral Decision-making, Forecasting, Game Theory and Role-play", *International Journal of Forecasting,* Vol.18, Issue3, pp 375-382, , July.

Jonathan Myers (1999), "Profits without Panic- Investment Psychology of Personal Wealth", Nicholas Brealey Publishing Ltd., pp169-180.

"World Wealth Grows to $33.3 trillion Says Merrill Lynch" (2006), Capgemini 2007 World Health Report" , 12th June.

Nivedita Chakravartty (2007), "For a Few Dollars More", *The Times of India,* 18th, Jan.

Rivkin, Annabel (2006), "How I make the Rich Richer",. *The Times of India,* 12th December.

Peter J Klein (1998), "Getting started in Security Analysis", John Wiley & Sons, pp 190-92

John W Schott & Jean S. Arbeiter (1998), "Mind over Money: Match your personality to a winning Financial Strategy", Little Brown publishers

Thomas Bailard, David Biehl and Ronald Kaiser, "Personal Money Management" (1986), 5th edn., Chicago Science Research Associate.

Kathleen Gurney (1988), "Your Money Personality: What It Is and How You Can Profit From It", Doubleday Books Pub.

Michael M. Pompian (2006), "Behavioral Finance and Wealth Management- How to Build Optimal Portfolios that Account for Investor Biases", John Wiley.

Kahneman and Tversky, Shafir Eldar (1979), "Preference, Belief and Similarity", MIT Press, pp.545-567.

Jan Annaert, Dries Heyman, Michèle Vanmaele, Sofieke Van Osselaer (2007), "Disposition Bias and Overconfidence in Institutional Trades", http://efmaefm.org/edhec-2008/dries.pdf.

Nelson Maina Waweru, Evelyne Munyoki, Enrico Uliana (2008), "The Effects of Behavioural Factors in Investment Decision-making: A Survey of Institutional Investors Operating at the Nairobi Stock Exchange", *International journal of Business and Emerging Markets,* Vol.1, No.1, pp. 24-37.

Richard L Peterson (2007), "Inside the Investor's Brain - The Power of Mind over Money", John Wiley & Sons, pp.266-267.

Fama, Eugene F. and Macbeth J. (1973), "*Risk, Return, and Equilibrium: Empirical Tests*", Journal of Political Economy, pp 279-281, May-June.

APPENDIX – I

Questionnaire

PART A

Please tick your choice in the relevant boxes:

1. Name (optional)
2. Age
   ( ) 18 – 30 ( ) 31 – 40
   ( ) 41 – 50 ( ) Above 50
3. Educational qualification
   ( ) Secondary level
   ( ) Higher Secondary level
   ( ) Graduate/Diploma
   ( ) Post-Graduate
   ( ) Professional
4. Profession
   ( ) Private ( ) Public
   ( ) Self-employed ( ) Business
   ( ) student ( ) --------(any other specify)
5. Experience in the field of investment
   ( ) less than 5 years
   ( ) 5 – 10 years
   ( ) 10 – 15 years
   ( ) 15 years & above
6. Tenure of investment
   ( ) Permanent possession of asset
   ( ) Long – term
   ( ) Intermediate
   ( ) short-term
   ( ) speculative
7. Investment Allocation
   ( ) real estate

() Gold/Silver
() Consumer durables n Mutual Funds
() Equity/Bonds/Debentures

8 Investor Category
() Fund Managers
() HNIs (High Networth Individuals)
() Retail Investors
() Intermediary Investors

9. Your Current value of Investments in shares and securities
() Less than Rs.500000
() Rs.500000 to Rs.10,00,000
() Rs.10,00,000 to Rs.15,00,000
() Above Rs.15,00,000

10. Basis for the choice of investment
() Industry
() Religion
() Management team
() Market Reaction

11. Your basic nature in investment decision is generally
() Cautious (Risk averse)
() Objective (Risk Neutral/ analytical)
() Optimistic (Risk Taker)

12. The main thing you will try to avoid in your investment program is
() Not owning the best performing types of investment
() Don't depend on either fundamental / Technical analysis of securities
() Trust only on my intuition.
() Over-reacting to the fears of uncertain times and the euphoria of good times.

13. Your expected rate of return is
() Above 50% () 50% to 40%
() 40% to 30% () 30% to 20%
() Below 20%

14. The rate of return you have earned is
() Above 40% () 40% to 30%
() 30% to 20% () 20% to 10%
() -10% to 10%

15. Your decisions on investment is based on
() My sole decision
() My peer group and friends' opinion
() My family/ spouse

15. Your decision is generally on
    - ( ) My instinct based on market movements
    - ( ) Technical Analysis made by myself
    - ( ) Advice taken from technical analyst

PART B

A few statements given below explains the behavior of investors. Please read carefully and tick the appropriate box, indicating how far you agree or disagree with these statements.

Strongly Agree - SA Agree - A No Opinion - NO
Disagree - D Strongly Disagree - SD

Q.No.	*Variables*	*SA*	*A*	*NO*	*D*	*SD*
1.	Investors continue to hold securities, they have personally selected					
2.	Investors love taking risk, to earn more returns					
3.	Investors always seek the advice of competent professional investors for selecting their investment					
4.	Investors have expert knowledge and vast experience in the stock market, that enables them to play safe always.					
5.	Investors frequently check the market values to confirm if they had picked the right stock/stocks					
6.	One should be diligent to respond to misleading signals quickly.					
7.	Several instances had made the investors learn from their past mistakes					
8.	I give more weightage for my views and opinions than the information I get while making my investment decisions.					
9.	I disregard risks that does not support my view					
10.	I tend to invest on my intuitive knowledge, ignoring to obtain complete information					
11.	I Invest in 'Bear' markets when my overall portfolio value declines					
12.	My investment is based on possible returns, even if they are uncertain					
13.	My choice is based on superior information; I need not know what information is available with the counter-party to trade					

Contd.

Q.No.	*Variables*	*SA*	*A*	*NO*	*D*	*SD*
14.	In a downturn share market, I believe that the market will bounce back					
15.	I am overly optimistic regarding future prospects followed by a successful investment experience					
16.	I pursue investments of high possible returns but low expected returns					
17.	I am a compulsive risk-seeker; I accept almost any degree of risk.					
18.	I am confident in my own skills and judgment in investing as distinct from others in the market, which proved successful in all my decisions					
19.	My intuition gives me strength and confidence to face the illusions and post judgment errors.					
20.	I will choose one of the investments with lower risk, when their expected returns are equal.					
21.	While risk taking for greater losses, or a sure loss, I would seek the chance to recover my money rather than getting profits.					
22.	I am not confident on the information I have obtained nor do I have the ability to process it.					
23.	The speed with which information is disseminated and investors' ability to mobilize funds, cause price trends					
24.	Investors will have a disposition to hold on to losing stocks and sell winners					
25.	I always make a complete and deep analysis of my potentials and available information before investing my funds.					
26.	Investors are not as diversified as they should be.					
27.	Investors have a lower propensity or intention to sell those stocks on which they have a capital loss					
28.	I am over confident about the future because of my ability to easily predict events					
29.	The investor knows that he is in a 'bubble'; it is advisable to stay in the market until it bursts					
30.	As a following agent, I choose the actions of the leading agents disregarding my own private information					
31.	I normally follow the crowd sentiment, due to convenience.					

Contd.

Q.No.	Variables	SA	A	NO	D	SD
32.	The group behavior implicates excess price volatility and affects the normalcy of the financial system.					
33.	Circuit breakers impose a trading halt in the face of substantial selling pressure to check the difference in interpretation, seems to be beneficial to the investors.					
34.	Experience and expertise in investments would lead to, more realistic and prompt investment.					
35.	Investors tend to over-react to negative information more zealously than to positive information.					
36.	Investors tend to follow the group, due to lack of confidence.					
37.	Investors trade on 'noise' (actions of others) as if it were information					
38.	Investors in some instances neglect their private information in order to trade against the market.					
39.	On any price changes or dividend announcements, the markets over-react or under-react					
40.	Volatility of IPO is due to lack of fixation of a mindset regarding the company.					
41.	A company recorded 20% earnings growth last quarter and expects a smaller growth rate this quarter. But if the company records a 40% growth rate in earnings, we may brush aside the growth rate as temporary.					
42.	Under-reaction enables smart managers a chance to buy the stock cheap, before market realizes the under-reaction					
43.	The heterogeneity in information processing capability is the main reason of the price and volume patterns observed in the market					
44.	Large investors are generally better informed than small investors					
45.	I read the documents accompanying an offer very carefully before my investment decision					
46.	Selling of loosing stocks than the winners is done on the month of December					
47.	Investors seek to buy 'hot 'stocks and try to avoid stocks which have performed poorly in the recent past					
48.	Investors assume that recent events will continue in the near future					
49.	One cannot avoid the error of judgment.					

PART C

Rank the investment according to your priority [In case, if you opt for Indirect investment]

i) Aggressive growth funds ________
ii) International stock funds ________
iii) Emerging growth funds ________
iv) Balanced funds ________
v) High -Yield bonds ________
vi) Short term convertible debentures ________
vii) Long term convertible debentures ________
viii) Growth and Income funds ________
ix) Money Market funds ________
x) Arbitrage funds ________